MW00637717

# I Killed for a Living

*Bross Deur, Vietnam, 1960.*

# I Killed for a Living

## The Story of the Last Big-Game Hunter in Southeast Asia

by

Etienne Oggeri

Safari Press

Oggeri, Etienne

Second edition

Safari Press

2010 Long Beach, California

ISBN 978-1-57157-339-1

Library of Congress Catalog Card Number: 2008927482

10 9 8 7 6 5 4 3 2 1

Printed in China

Readers wishing to receive the Safari Press catalog, featuring many fine books on big-game hunting, wingshooting, and sporting firearms, should write to Safari Press Inc., P.O. Box 3095, Long Beach, CA 90803, USA. Tel: (714) 894-9080 or visit our Web site at www.safaripress.com.

I dedicate this book to my wife Lechi, my muse, who has always believed in my talent as a narrator and encouraged me to write my stories. Her presence by my side during many of my big-game hunts made them unforgettable.

This book is also dedicated to dear friends from my childhood, my hunting companions François Da Cruz (deceased) and his brother Jean; Henri Portier (deceased) and his brother Alain; and La Quy Dac, who provided me with photographs of our hunts, thus enlivening my stories.

And finally, in a book on my life as a hunter, it would be unforgivable if I did not mention my friends and brothers, Montagnard trackers An Nga, K'Loi, K'Lan, K'Sou, and K'War (all deceased), the best trackers in South Vietnam and faithful companions on my hunts of yesteryear.

# Table of Contents

# Preface

This book is very likely to be the last one on big-game hunting in Vietnam since I am the last professional hunter and guide alive. I left that country in 1962. Since the war, which ended in 1975 with the reunification of North and South Vietnam, big-game hunting has become illegal.

My book, however, will bring to the passionate big-game hunter a glimpse of the paradise that was Vietnam before the war. Readers can imagine the jungles in which wild animals roamed and the hunters who went after them, following the tracks of the most coveted trophies, the tiger and the gaur (Indian bison).

The photographs in this book are very rare, for they depict the mountain tribes, called the Moïs—those hospitable inhabitants of the forests who have disappeared forever. You will never meet them in their indigo sarongs or *trousse-couilles* with a small *navaja* (knife) in their long hair knotted on top of their heads; their ears pierced and adorned with bamboo or ivory plates four inches in diameter; their necks, arms, and ankles covered with copper necklaces and bracelets; and their teeth filed to fine points. The Moïs of Old Vietnam no longer exist. They have been assimilated into the Vietnamese population and have adopted the customs and ways of life of the city people. You will no longer see a bare-breasted young Moïesse (Montagnard woman) walking to the river along a forest trail.

Young readers, curious about a bygone past, will find this evocation interesting. Old readers who have known life in the jungles of Vietnam will be happy to revive their dreams of youth.

Many books have been written on big-game hunting. Their authors, however, tend to mention only Africa and India; consequently, very few reliable books have been written on Indochina. These include *Les Grands Animaux Sauvages de l'Annam*, published in 1930 and written by Fernand Millet, an expert on hunting; *Les Grandes Chasses en Indochine*, by A. Plas, the only known professional hunter there from 1930 to 1945; and *La Faune et la Flore Indochinoises* by de Monestrol.

The few other books I have been able to find are the works of amateurs who knew nothing about the people, the animals, and big-game hunting. They were officials of the French administration of that time, or employees of business companies, or a province chief who was lucky enough to shoot at close range a panther trapped by the natives of the region. A very small number of authors tried to impress their readers with scientific or pedantic words that said little. As a result, very few people read those books, and most hunters did not realize what they could have found in Vietnam, Cambodia, and Laos, the three countries that formed French Indochina. Very often I heard people say, "*En Indochine beaucoup de gibier nulle part, très peu ou rien partout*" (In Indochina a lot of game nowhere, very little game or nothing everywhere.)

The occasional hunters of that time mostly got their guns out after a good dinner and several drinks. Comfortably seated in their cars, driven by a friend or a chauffeur, they went to the edge of the forests where they perhaps shot at close range the unlucky deer, male or female, attracted by the beam of their headlights.

The real hunter was the one who could walk thirty or forty kilometers (up to twenty-five miles) a day through uneven terrain, wade through swamps infested with leeches, or swim across swift mountain torrents. He was like a jungle animal himself. The mountain tribes recognized him and welcomed him among them. For days he would share their frugal life. He loved hunting not so much for the trophy but for the excitement of the chase. I was that kind of passionate hunter. I was always in the jungle on the trail of wild animals in the company of my faithful Moïs, with whom I felt more relaxed than I did with the city people we call civilized.

Most people think of wild animals as being dangerous. They talk about their ferocity, their cruelty, and say they charge at you without being attacked and they kill without provocation. I can tell you that during my whole career as a hunter, I was attacked only a few times, and each time, I provoked the animal.

If you have the opportunity, examine those beasts we call savage, after you have succeeded in killing them. You will discover that their bodies are covered with the scars of ancient wounds, and sometimes their wounds are recent. Almost always they have been hurt in the stomach or have broken bones. As a result of such experiences, many of them resulting from encounters with humans, they will run from man until the moment they realize they can no longer escape the two-legged creature. Then they turn to face their aggressor and charge. Into that desperate attempt to avoid death, they put all their anger. That is why people describe at length the bloody madness of an elephant, gaur, or buffalo. Those animals do not charge man himself but rather the human scent that forewarns them of impending doom.

The man-eating tiger is very likely to be a tiger handicapped by an old wound that prevents him from hunting, or he is too old and too weak to go after other animals. Of all the creatures, man is the weakest, devoid of natural defenses, and his flesh is tender.

During my hunting years I killed many animals. I am not going to boast about the great number of wild beasts whose lives I ended because now I am ashamed and I want to forget them. I once loved hunting passionately, but now I hate the memory of it. When I can, I avoid killing; even a fly or an ant is safe in my home.

Even during my hunting years, in spite of the excitement of the chase, remorse clouded the pride of my victories. As a young boy, I asked for forgiveness from the birds I killed. Later, as a professional hunter, I asked my victims to forgive me; my joy in the kill was never complete. I felt, however, a link of understanding between the wild animals and myself.

When I worked as an intelligence research analyst in the Fourth Battalion of Psychological Warfare in Fort Bragg, North Carolina, I was invited to hunt deer on the forest reserve of the base. I saw many animals run away from me, but I was never able to shoot at them. Something stopped me from pressing the trigger. I saw in the eyes of my host his disappointment at seeing the professional hunter he knew I had been letting a coveted deer escape. I was not able to explain to him that remorse over my former "crimes" had killed the hunter in me.

I guess, however, that remorse is like love. Not everyone can feel it. So this book is not an attempt to influence anyone. My point is to share with you my experience as a former professional big-game hunter who passionately loved his job and did it well. This is all being said without boasting. My legacy, then, is the story I am about to tell of the hunting paradise that was French Indochina in days before Vietnam descended into an inferno of corruption, war, and atrocity.

Many pictures in the following pages have been sent to me by old friends; other illustrations are oil paintings done by my wife Lechi, a former hunter like myself and now an artist. My own collection of films and photographs was confiscated when I was deported from Vietnam in 1962, so I have had to rely on the kindness of others for the artwork that illustrates this book.

# Acknowledgments

To my wife, Lechi, for translating my manuscript, which was written in French. She alone was able to decipher my handwriting and type it. Since she is a talented artist, she has also reproduced some of my old photographs and transformed them into magnificent oil paintings.

My grateful thanks also to Professor Janet Cavano for her careful editing of the English version.

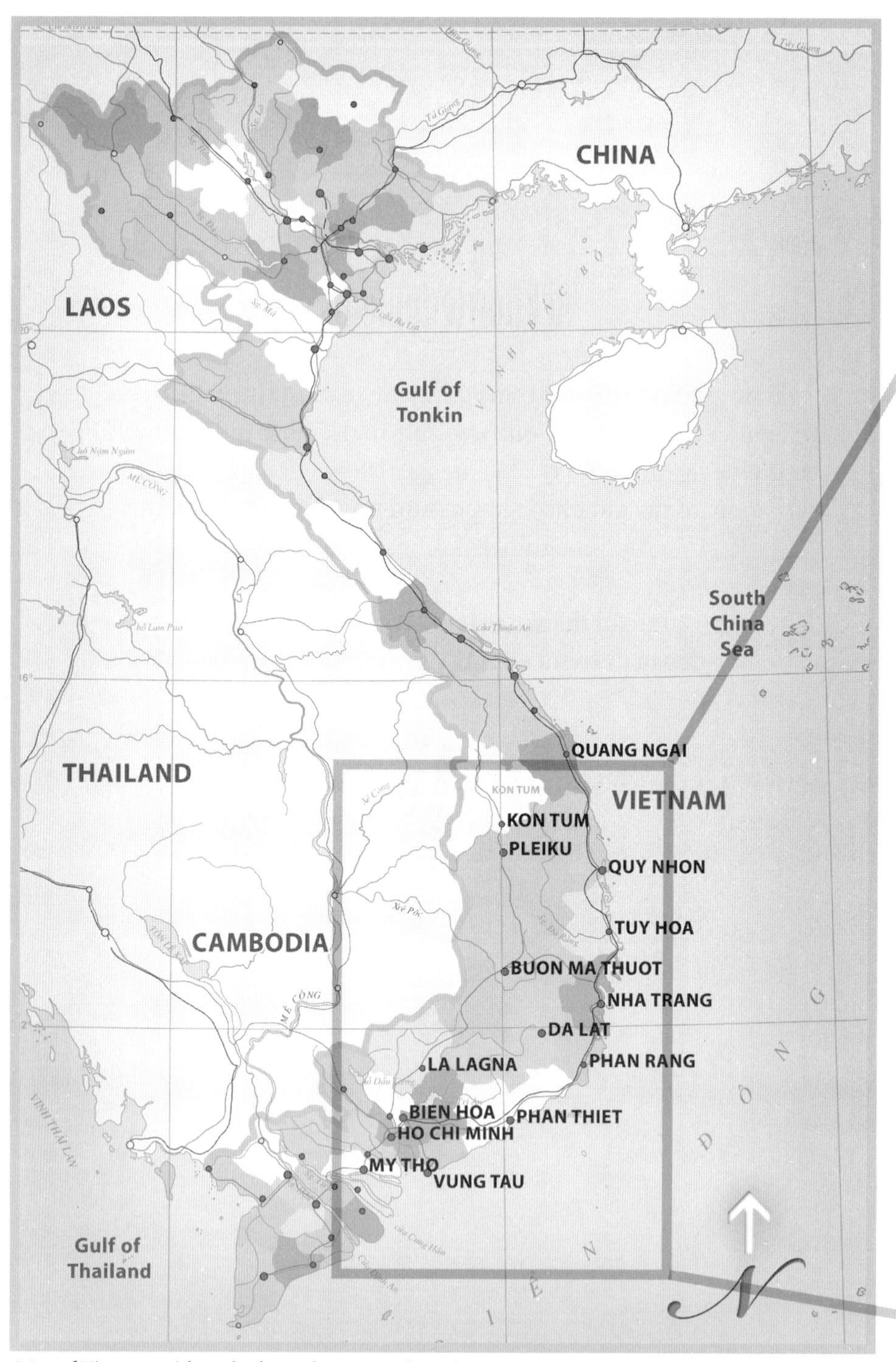


*Map of Vietnam with author's marks. Inset enlarged on next page.*

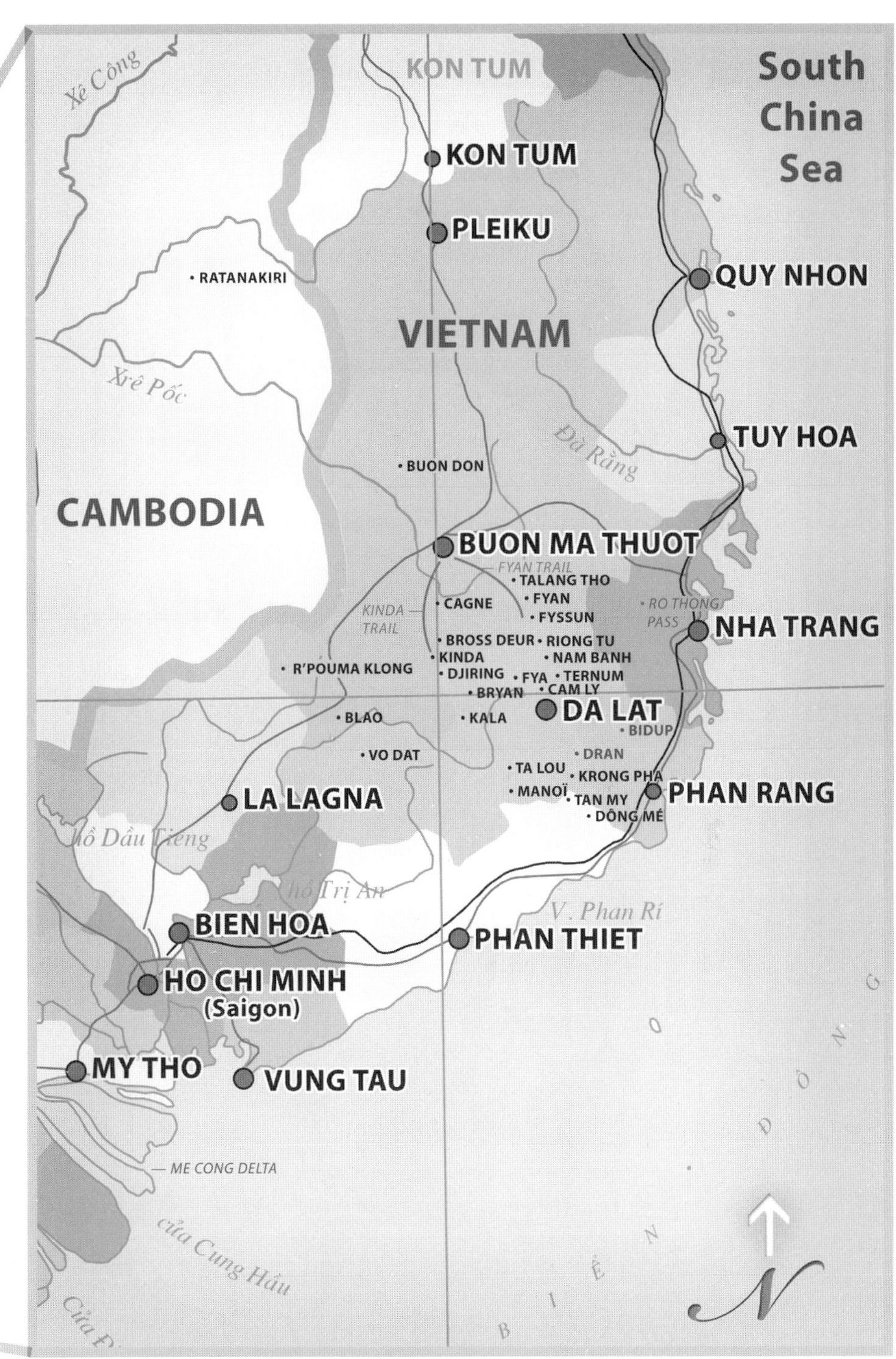


*Locations of author's travels, close-up of map on page xiv.*

# Seasons and Climate of Vietnam

## Chapter 1

There are really only two seasons in Vietnam: the dry season from November to May and the monsoon the rest of the year. For months it rains almost every day. I never recommended that season to foreign tourists who planned to hunt here. They would not have been able to withstand the bad weather even if they were in good physical condition. Most of my clients were not in their prime, and they would not have enjoyed being soaked every day from morning until night. I always advised them to plan their trip for the dry season.

For the professional hunter who lived from the product of his hunts, however, the rainy season was the best time of the year. The footprints made by the animals were easily visible in the mud and facilitated the work of the trackers. Moreover, the animals' senses were not so acute then as during the dry season. We could approach them more easily, thanks especially to the fact that the wet leaves littering the trails did not crunch under our feet. I always took advantage of the monsoon to gather trophies and sell them to tourists or unlucky hunters.

My hunting areas on the Lang Bian plateau extended from the town of Da Lat to milestone 113 on the highway to Saigon, from Da Lat to Ban-Dong along the jungle trails of Fyan and Kinda, and from Da Lat to Krong Pha. These regions were easily accessible to tourists even during the period of intense heat. Sometimes the hot summers in Vietnam were a hindrance for foreign hunters who were not used to walking for a long distance in the heat, which was necessary to find the elephant and the gaur. Since I was familiar with those hunting areas, I knew the grazing grounds of the herds, and the *dâtches* (salt licks) where they came to get the minerals they needed early in the morning or late in the afternoon. My knowledge of the land allowed me to spare my clients long walks through rough terrain in search of fresh tracks.

My favorite areas for hunting gaur and tiger were the Lang Bian plateau between Cam Ly and Fyan, and the Djiring plateau as far as Cagne. There we could find the best specimens of these animals. Other interesting areas were the Blao province, stretching to the plain of R'Pouma Klong, and the vast plain of Krong Pha as far as Ca Na. They were the best places for big-game hunting, but the great walking distance to them and the lack of bearers made access difficult. Once a hunter reached them and set up his camp, however, he was in a hunting paradise where all the small and big game he could want, including birds, were within a walk of only five to ten miles.

We could find banteng (wild oxen), wild Asiatic buffalo, elephant, gaur, panther, and tiger in the plain of R'Pouma Klong and the great plain of Krong Pha to Dong Mé, but the furs of the felines there were not so beautiful as those of the wild cats on the Lang Bian Plateau, where it was colder.

The best regions for elephant were R'Pouma Klong, Cagne, Krong Pha, all in Krong Pha going toward Mont Bidup, Song Mao, and Ratanakiri (province of Cambodia) not too far from Ban Dong and Ban Me Thuot. It was easy to cross the border if one was willing to risk being caught entering illegally.

I was not afraid of illegality when I was on the trail of an elephant adorned with heavy tusks. Ivory had always fascinated me, and, stimulated by the desire to possess a pair of magnificent tusks, I was fearless.

When I hunted there or in Ban Dong, I was incognito. I took my bearers and trackers with me from Lang Bian and reached the border by avoiding all the neighboring villages. We set up our temporary camp in a dry river where we knew of a small creek with fresh water, and where a canopy of giant bamboo protected us from the glaring sun. From there I scouted the area without any problems, thanks to my Jeep equipped with a winch.

Every year I obtained an "A" permit for big-game hunting, which allowed me to go where I wanted and shoot two elephants, for which I had to pay the killing taxes. In order to get more trophies without having problems with the government, however, I paid for two or three additional permits in the names of friends who did not hunt. I could have tried to make more profit by avoiding taxes, but when I killed an elephant near a village, I could not hide it. So I had to give it to the villagers after taking the tusks, and I also had to pay a tax for it.

It was a good thing I mostly respected the law because one day I was arrested by a group of French agents of the National Security in charge of protecting Emperor Bao Dai against the Viet Minh, whose presence had been signaled in the area. The guerrillas were not very active, however, because they were there on the High Plateau only for propaganda purposes or to convalesce.

The emperor still ruled over Vietnam, although the French allowed him very limited powers. Because he did not have much to do, he devoted most of his time to pursuing women and wild animals. He had problems with neither. The women flocked to him because of his high position and his money, and he killed his tiger from the back of his favorite elephant. He was a big-game-hunting fanatic and considered the High Plateau as his personal reserve.

I was handcuffed and brought before him in his camp. He was taking his breakfast surrounded by a small group of courtiers. He eyed me from head to foot, had the handcuffs removed, and simply offered me an apple. Then he asked me why I hunted in his reserve. I answered that I was not aware that the place was an imperial reserve since it was not indicated on my permit. Besides, there were not many hunters in that area, which was rich in game of all kind. He started laughing and said, "All right, continue your hunt in my reserve. I give you the permission, but leave my tigers alone."

I thanked him and continued to hunt with his permission—but not for long. He was toppled a few months later by a eunuch who, as it turned out, had considerable balls.

All the regions mentioned above were my favorite hunting grounds for elephant and tiger—partly because I was practically the only hunter there. I took advantage of that fact to kill more than the authorized quota. I also confess that I did not always pay the right killing taxes, because they were very high. Between the taxes, the bribes to village chiefs, and the normal safari expenses, I would have earned next to nothing from my hunts. I preferred to take the risk and pay little or nothing. I was the rebellious poacher. However, I consider myself less blameworthy than the respected professional "white hunters" of Africa and India such as Walter Bell, John Hunter, "Pondoro" Taylor, Marcus Daly, Jim Corbett, and others who killed in one day more elephants than I did in one year. Males and females fell under the bullets of those great "nimrods" known and admired by the world's hunters. I was only a poacher watched closely by the French and Vietnamese administration.

People also conducted big-game hunts on elephant-back in Ban Dong, Ratanakiri, and all the province of Dar Lac. Clients who wanted that kind of hunt had to pay extra money. The hunter perched in his basket atop the elephant could go long distances without becoming tired and kill his tiger without danger. This also gave him the aura of an important person, since the royal family of England would hunt the same way in the savannas of India. The only difference was that in India, hundreds of beaters chased the tiger in front of them, whereas in Ban-Dong the hunter would shoot the tiger running before his elephant, which served as both the transportation and the beater.

In all the regions I have mentioned, hunters could be sure of success. In the years 1930–1960 we could still hunt banteng and sometimes elephant from the road going from Krong Pha to Ca Na. After 1960 the big game learned to retreat far into the jungles. People had to walk great distances because there were no vehicle tracks. The thought of having to walk thirty or forty kilometers (up to twenty-five miles) before finding a village and guides cooled them down. Moreover, it was very easy to get lost in those vast plains where in the dry season almost all the creeks were dried up and water was scarce.

A few years after the war ended in 1975, the new regime in Vietnam created a reserve zone, a national park. The place chosen for it was the famous plain of R'Pouma Klong, a three-day walk from Blao or the River Da Huai. Alas, the war devastated the country's big-game populations, thanks to the widespread use of napalm and other defoliants, and the fact that most of the villagers had weapons (Garand .30-06 rifles and AK-47s).

Intensive clearing of the land for cultivation was another factor. Vietnam could not have become a world producer of coffee without the clearing of thousands of acres of forests. The government made the situation worse by allowing the cutting down of oak forests to generate the charcoal used by both the urban and rural populations, as in Haiti.

Man needs land to live, and naturally his needs come first before those of the wild animals. His land clearing endangers the animal world. Since large stretches of savanna do not exist in Vietnam, the animals cannot find refuge and shelter, as can the animals that live on the plains of Africa and India. Until 1960, however, a hunter accompanied by a good guide could in three weeks shoot creatures ranging from the francolin to the elephant. He could even get two different trophies the same day.

Vietnam is no longer the hunting paradise that I once knew and loved. One of my friends, a passionate hunter like myself, said to me after visiting the country a few years ago, "Even the monkeys have disappeared. The forests of Dâu, Ban Lang, and the great bamboo no longer exist. Along the roads you can see only *bidonvilles* (hot towns where houses have tin roofs)." Disappointed, he decided not to return to the Vietnam we had loved so much and where we had lived the best years of our lives.

# Animal Life of Indochina 1930–1960

## Chapter 2

## Medium-Size Game

*Sambar or Aristotle deer.* The antlers of this animal take various shapes, depending on their habitat. Some individuals have small and misshapen antlers; in others the antlers are well developed and perfectly symmetrical. The male is usually 1.4 meters (4½ feet) tall at the withers and, empty of its entrails, weighs about 200 kilos (440 pounds). It lives either alone or with a herd of five to eight others. The sambar has dark gray/brown hair and grows new, velvety antlers in August, when the deer season opens. Velvet horn was and is highly prized as an aphrodisiac by Asians. These animals come out at night and can be found at dusk and dawn in forest clearings, rice fields, and swamps. People would usually hunt them with the help of an electric or carbide lamp. These deer make ideal bait for tiger. Both males and females often have an open sore on their throats, a kind of ulcer of the skin.

*Eld deer.* The shoulder height of an adult male Eld deer is 1.2 meters (4 feet). Its live weight can reach 100 kilos (220 pounds). The antlers end in the shape of a hand with four fingers. The hair of old adult males is dark brownish-yellow. These animals used to live in great numbers in herds of ten to twenty in the pine forests and hills surrounding Da Lat, on the high plateau of Lang Bian, and in Cagne, Ban Dong, and Krong Pha until 1944. The population dwindled from 1944 to 1962, but by 1947 Eld deer no longer existed in Da Lat on the plateau of Lang Bian.

Epizootic disease affected the Eld deer, but their disappearance from the Lang Bian hills was largely due to the hunts organized by some old colonists whose minds had deteriorated from their daily intake of alcoholic beverages. These men would bet on the number of deer they could kill from their cars during one night's hunt with an electric lamp. They decimated the animals, shooting males and females indiscriminately with guns loaded with buckshot, taking their tails as trophies and leaving the bodies to rot. Moreover, Japanese soldiers, who occupied Da Lat after their coup of 9 March 1945, treated the herds of Eld deer as their pantry: They often went to the hills to gather fresh deer meat.

I still remember that long-ago time when tourists from Saigon would visit the Da Lat hills to admire the herds of those pretty animals, which became accustomed to the friendly presence of the people. The deer were the ornament of our pine forests.

*Swamp deer.* Another rare species is the swamp deer. Much appreciated for its meat and velvety antlers, it looks like a small sambar, and its whistlelike cry could be heard at night. It lived and fed in rice fields and in swamps.

*Muntjac.* This animal is also known as the barking deer, but the name most used by the French in Vietnam was "con man," from the Vietnamese *con mån* [barking deer]. The muntjac is small, with a dark brown head and neck, but the rest of its body is orange-yellow and its belly is white. The male is 60 to 80 centimeters (23 to 31 inches) tall and weighs 40 kilos (about 80 pounds). The muntjac, which has well-developed upper canines, is highly solitary except during the mating season.

The *grandicornis* muntjac or giant muntjac, a very rare subspecies, has golden fur. Unlike its more common cousin, which lives in forest clearings and pine forests, the *grandicornis* hides in dense, humid, and dark rain forests. It is taller and heavier than the common muntjac. I was able to kill a beautiful trophy *grandicornis* during my 1961 hunt with Berry B. Brooks (see chapter 16). The animal was one meter (about 40 inches) high at the withers and weighed 60 kilos (130 pounds). In my whole career as a hunter, I shot only three *grandicornis*, and each encounter occurred on the edges of dense and humid forests. I believe that I have in my collection of trophies from Indochina the only record trophy of a giant muntjac.

In 1998 the Office of Hunting Reserves in Vietnam announced that it had discovered a very rare new deer species, apparently never shot before and seemingly unknown to hunters. It was no other than the *grandicornis* muntjac. In his book titled *Les Grands Animaux Sauvages de l'Annam* and published in 1930, Fernand Millet, a well-known hunter, had mentioned that extremely rare deer. So did Louis Chochod in his book *La Faune Indochinoise* in 1910. Thus, our *grandicornis* was already known in the distant past, but the only people to have seen it, much less to have shot it, were the very few fanatic hunters who would walk in the humid, leech-infested forests to get a glimpse of it.

*Wild boar.* There is only one kind of wild boar in Vietnam, the maned or India boar. Looking much like the boar found in Europe, it usually stands one meter (40 inches) high at the withers and weighs about 200 kilos (440 pounds).

Some hunters insist that Vietnam holds another kind of wild boar that looks very much like the domestic Montagnard hog. In my opinion, these animals are merely the product of a wild boar mating with a domesticated female.

*Plantigrades* are animals that walk on the sole of the foot with the heel touching the ground, such as bears or humans). The one most often seen is the *ours cochon* [hog bear]. It has shiny, black, short fur with an orange-yellow collar. The male is about 1.2 meters long (4 feet) and weighs up to 60 kilos (132 pounds). Another species, called *ours des cocotiers* (coconut-tree bear), looks like the first one but is smaller—60 centimeters (about 2 feet) long and weighing 20 kilos (45 pounds). It is not aggressive and is easily tamed. Both species exist mostly in Southeast Asia.

A third plantigrade is the Tibetan bear or Asian black bear. It is bigger than the first two and has thick black fur with a yellow collar like the others. An adult male is 2 meters (6½ feet) long and weighs 200 kilos (440 pounds). It feeds on fruits, honey, and vegetables, but will also feed on baits intended for tiger—it eats rotten or fresh meat without hesitation. It is very dangerous when wounded or cornered. I believe that all three species still exist.

I witnessed a drama while trying to film one of these bears. The guide who was with me had his spear and I had my 8mm Mauser. We were waiting in a *ray* (mountain rice field), hidden on a platform that served as an observation post where villagers could watch their crops and fend off raids by monkeys and other beasts. Eventually we saw a huge bear seated on a big rock eating the villagers' cucumbers and melons. It was only 10 meters (about 35 feet) from us and was not aware of our presence.

I was getting ready to film *Ursus thibetanus* when my guide jumped from the platform and ran toward the animal with his spear raised to punish it for its thievery. The animal merely looked at him and continued to eat. The guide thrust his spear into its stomach and was about to do it again when the bear seized him and crushed his skull with its teeth. I shot, but not quickly enough. The guide fell dead next to the sweet-looking bear.

The Tibetan bear is now considered a rare species, like *ours cochon* and *ours des cocotiers.* Today they can be seen only in zoos. Their gall bladder is an important element in Asian medicine, which may be the reason the plantigrades have become so rare. They have been poached pitilessly.

# Small Game

Small animals and reptiles were very abundant in certain regions of Vietnam. Monkeys, civets, small wild cats called *chats tigres* (tiger cats) or *chats panthères* (panther cats), ocelots, flying squirrels, wild dogs, a few lizards, and snakes could be found everywhere.

Generally people shot the small land-based game whenever they encountered it. Back then I would not advise hunters to take their hunting dogs with them. Leeches infested the humid areas where small game was found. The poor dogs, with their muzzles close to the ground to sniff the tracks of possible prey, would themselves become the prey of leeches, which would stick themselves to the inside of the hounds' noses.

Many of the reptiles, like the pythons, were not poisonous. Among the poisonous ones were the king cobra, the krait, green vipers, and banana snakes (small green vipers). All of them existed in great numbers in the R'Pouma Klong plain, and hunters would encounter them every day. I shot a few cobras that were 4 meters (13 feet) long. The villagers of those regions preferred cobra meat to deer meat. One of my guides said that in certain villages people avoided eating deer meat because of superstition, based on beliefs he could not explain.

A great American hunter, Col. Charles Askins, mentioned in one of his books on Indochina that he had seen cobras 18 feet long. A friend of mine, son of the well-known hunter, Plas, killed a cobra 6 meters (about 19 feet) in length in his hunting camp on the bank of the Da-Dung River in the Bross Deur area.

There were many hares (wrongly called wild rabbits) that were smaller than the European hares. They did not live in burrows. People would shoot them at night with the aid of headlamps. This kind of hunting was not forbidden then.

Small game also included birds—peacocks, silver and golden pheasants, *épéroniers* and *argus*, francolin (red partridge, cousins of the *bartavelles* or gray partridge, and wild chickens that look very much like their domestic cousins but are smaller and have brighter colors). The best places for birds were the plateau of Djiring, Lang Bian, and the great plain of Krong Pha to the border of Ca Na. One could find them everywhere, especially in bamboo forests, clearings, and rice fields after the harvest when the ground was littered with seed. They lived in coveys of eight to fifteen birds—two or three young roosters along with hens and an old rooster characterized by long, colorful tail feathers. Those resplendent feathers could be one meter (39 inches) long.

There were also hazel-grouse called wood-partridge, which lived in coveys of eight to ten birds. Their meat was a delight. Other birds, called columbines, included turtledoves, green doves (the size of domestic pigeons with apple-green feathers and red legs), "ma" doves (bigger than the turtledoves), *ramiers,* and ring doves.

Vietnam's water birds included snipe, found in great quantities to the south of Saigon on the Lang Bian Plateau and in North Vietnam. Less numerous were woodcock, teal and other wild ducks, and geese found to the north of Tonkin.

## Big Game

At that time the largest animals in Vietnam consisted of elephant, tiger, gaur, Asiatic water buffalo, banteng, and even bear (covered in the section on "Medium-Size Game" earlier in this chapter). There was also the spotted panther, nebulous panther, and *panthère dorée* (golden panther), which was also called the "temmincki" panther. In Cambodia and Laos one could find another bovine, the kouprey, a wild cattle that looks somewhat between a cross of a banteng and a gaur but in reality is a completely different species. Javan rhinoceros (the two-horned kind) existed but were very rare, found only in Cambodia and Laos. During my entire career as a hunter I never saw one, but I happened upon fresh tracks, which I had to abandon because they were headed toward a Viet Cong command post.

In the opinion of many great hunters of that period, the gaur and the tiger were the most beautiful Indochinese trophies. They are indeed impressive and striking. Every foreign hunter went after these two. For me, the tiger is the number one trophy in the world. My vote for second place goes to the jaguar of South America.

To end my chapter on the fauna of Indochina, I will talk about the big cats, the elephant, and the bovines one could (and probably still can) find in that wonderful part of the world. I hunted them in the plains of R'Pouma Klong and Krong Pha, the plateaus of Djiring and Cagne, from Da Lat to Fyan and Ban Me Thuot, and in Bidup, the hunting paradise of Pierre Chanjou, an old friend, hunter, and professional guide.

# Elephant

Smaller than the African elephant, the handsome Asian elephant can reach 10 or 11 feet at the shoulder as an adult. Its tusks rarely weigh over 20 kilos (44 pounds) the pair. There are, however, some exceptions. I shot a 12-foot-tall elephant with exceptional tusks: They were 7 feet long and together weighed over 50 kilos (110 pounds).

Mr. Leleu, an engineer of public works, wanted to try a last hunt on elephant back in the province of Ban Dong toward Ratanakiri in Cambodia before returning to France for his retirement. He shot his first and last animal, an elephant carrying tusks of 80 kilos (176 pounds) the pair. They were registered at the Wildlife office at Ban Me Thuot, as confirmed by a Mr. Coudoux, a security officer.

My friend Jean Da Cruz shot another fine bull with tusks weighing 52 kilos (114 pounds) the pair in the Dam Rong area near Ban Me Thuot with the help of a Montagnard guide who was a very good tracker. These beautiful trophies came into the possession of Ngo Van Chi, a Vietnamese hunter who organized hunts for Ngo Dinh Nhu, the brother and adviser of Ngo Dinh Diem, president of Vietnam from 1954 to 1963.

Ngo Van Chi had hired my friend Da Cruz and his guide for that hunt. He promised Da Cruz a secondhand rifle, a Mauser 9.3x62, and some money for his guide. Once he had the ivory, though, he did not pay either my friend or his guide. Chi was never honest in his deals, and all the trophies he displayed in his house had been bought. I knew who shot them. That big-game hunter shot only snipes. Certain American hunters had wrongly praised Chi and his hunts, while he spent his time harassing people who were unlucky enough to have borrowed money from him.

I knew him very well. I took him on his first night hunt in Fyan (Lang Bian Plateau) in 1949. We often hunted together. I was very young then, just graduated from the lycée [high school]. I did not have a car to transport game, so Chi let me use his old Jeep—for a certain amount of money; he also took half the profit brought by the game I shot.

I drove the Jeep, hunted, and sold the meat. Chi did nothing but cash his share of the money. After some time our association ended. Chi told people that his passion in hunting was the pleasure of going after the prey, not doing it for money, as I did. I did not hesitate to tell him what I thought of him. This infuriated him, and he did his best to cause me harm. Since he had the friendship of the president's brother, the harm done was great.

He told the brother that I was working for France's Military Intelligence and the CIA. The government used that information as a pretext to expel me from the country since it could not give the real reason for that arbitrary decision—which was my romance with the sister of Madame Nhu, the first lady. Many years later, in 1989, I heard from Chi. He had come to the United States as a refugee. He was getting old and living on American welfare.

# Tiger

The tiger (*cop* in Vietnamese, *k'liou* in Montagnard) is the world's most beautiful trophy. The African lion, king of the savannas, is not comparable to its peer of the bamboo forests. In my opinion no trophy matches the magnificence of the tiger. In India in colonial times it was the game reserved for members of the royal family of England when they felt like hunting, whence came the expression "the regal tiger hunt." Today the tiger population in Vietnam is greatly diminished with only a few remaining in the most remote corners of the country.

A big adult male is between 2.80 and 3.30 meters (between 9 and 11 feet) from tip of nose to tip of tail and weighs 250 to 300 kilos (550 to 660 pounds). There are rare exceptions. I shot a few specimens 3.50 meters (11½ feet) long.

In 1968 the Fayetteville *Observer*, a newspaper in North Carolina, told the story of a tiger that entered the American military base in Khe Sanh, Vietnam. The Khe Sanh area was well known for the fierce battles between U.S. Marines and the North Vietnamese guerrillas who surrounded them during the war. There were terrible losses of lives on both sides. At the end of one such confrontation, the tiger—attracted by the smell of the blood of the wounded and dead—was found prowling about the base. The marines killed it with bursts of M16 carbine fire.

That tiger was colossal, 13 feet long from muzzle to end of tail and weighing 500 pounds. I heard of only one other really enormous cat. Plas, a well-known professional hunter of Djiring, South Vietnam, guided one of his clients to a huge tiger that was 12½ feet long. Cats that large are extremely rare.

The tiger and the gaur are my favorite trophies. The tiger, found everywhere in Indochina (Laos, Cambodia, Vietnam) back then, is striking in its power, agility, and beauty. The hair varies from light yellow to dark orange, with black stripes on the back and white on the chest and belly. No two animals have exactly the same striping pattern.

In spite of its weight, this animal is unbelievably agile. The colossal strength of its front legs and jaws allows it to drag a 300-pound deer easily. I saw a tiger drag a female gaur weighing more than 800 kilos (1,700 pounds) for 100 meters, and another move an elephant a few meters to the shade of a clump of bamboo where the cat could enjoy its huge meal. In spite of its extraordinary strength, however, it seldom attacked man, doing so only when wounded or too old to tackle its normal large prey. A tiger would not hesitate to follow a herd of elephants for several days if it smelled the presence of young among them or the scent of a female about to bring forth a baby.

Tigers are prudent and suspicious. Their survival instinct and alertness warn them of danger. This makes hunting them somewhat less dangerous but more difficult. Their sense of smell is not keen because they often eat rotten meat. I do not mean to compare them to French gourmets who love to eat the aged meat of partridge or snipe, but most of the tiger's prey consists of big animals and they cannot eat the whole thing at one time. They finish their meals over several days, and meat rots quickly in tropical countries. Their mouths become infected by the putrefaction of their food, and the infection dulls their sense of smell.

Once, I had a tiger wander around my blind without being able to detect my presence. Yet my smell was strong since I had rubbed my body with citronella oil to repel the insects of the forests. The cat passed in front of the blind several times, sniffing, but never noticed the strange scent.

On the other hand, though the tiger's sense of smell is limited, its sight and hearing are well developed. A human seldom sees a cat first—the tiger sees and hears before being seen. Its principal activities are hunting and hiding. It likes dark and dense spots and uneven terrain. Its favorite resting places are in bamboo forests and among latanier trees, though it will negotiate any kind of terrain day or night when hunting.

The tiger almost always hunts by night, visiting pastures, small clearings, and the swamps frequented by sambar deer. Sometimes it prowls through villages and catches a dog or a pig—or even a young buffalo if it is quite hungry and ready to risk the horns of the mother. During periods of famine the tiger is satisfied with a python, frog, porcupine, or even a peacock imprudent enough to perch on a low branch for the night.

The tiger would eat a human if the person were handicapped by a wound or weakened by old age. It would prowl around Montagnard villages by day or by night and take the opportunity to jump on a child or even an adult relieving himself in the woods. Such an attack would so arouse the terror of the villagers that they would ask a passing hunter to kill the predator.

There were man-eaters in South Vietnam, especially the northern regions of Pleiku and Kon Tum. According to the reports of Montagnard hunters, tigers would find dead or wounded Viet Minh soldiers hidden in the brush during the French–Viet Minh War, 1945–1954, and eat them before medical teams could find and take them to the hospital. The animals came to associate a good meal with the noise of cannons and bursts of machine-gun fire. They were like the sharks of Poulo Condor Island [Con Dao Island today], which arrived at the sound of the death gong to feast on the corpses of political prisoners thrown into the sea after they died from illness or mistreatment.

In the opinion of many hunters, the tiger is really dangerous only when it is wounded or cornered. Most hunters of other game would choose to abandon their preferred prey rather than follow it in the dense forests of bamboo or latanier, or crawl after it in swamps covered with mangroves. Not many hunters could stay cool in front of a charging tiger. They would have to shoot fast and not miss because a wounded tiger will charge with lightning speed, close to the ground, and will claw open a belly and drag the entrails with it.

Although I understood their reluctance to follow a wounded cat, I did not agree with their decision to let a wounded animal die in excruciating pain in the middle of a dense forest or thick swamp, hidden from the sight of its pursuers. The very few who dared to go after a wounded cat reported that the tiger announced its final charge by a raging, raucous growl. Sometimes the tiger would make a detour and attack from behind, as happened to me more than once.

If you decide to be among the few daring hunters, remember that you should always be alone in pursuing a wounded wild beast, so that no one will be in front of or behind you. A real professional hunter will never agree to be accompanied by his client, especially a nervous one. He will allow only a tracker he can trust to follow him. He must otherwise be alone and listen to every noise, follow the blood trail left by the wounded animal, and observe carefully the traces of its progress.

People usually hunt tigers from a blind camouflaged with bamboo and *tranh* grass, usually twenty meters (sixty-five feet) from a bait solidly attached to a tree. A tiger almost always finds the bait within three days because the presence of vultures or crows is a telling sign of the "feast." The animal comes and assuages its immediate hunger, then hides in the bush nearby until ready for its next meal.

The hunter, informed by his trackers that the bait has been visited, gets inside the blind with his gun, a headlight, a Thermos of coffee, and his blanket. The trackers leave him, talking loudly as they go to make the animal believe that no one remains to bother it during its repast. Before getting settled in the blind, the hunter checks the ground to make sure that the only tracks around the bait are a tiger's paw prints; if wild dogs or boars have found the bait and started to eat, a tiger will seldom approach and it would be a waste of time to wait for it.

The appearance of a tiger on the bait can easily make a hunter nervous. He should calm down and concentrate on synchronizing his movements. He must wait until the animal starts to eat before taking aim through the blind's opening and shooting, twice if necessary. He should avoid shooting at the head, which is a key element of the trophy. When the guide hears the shot, he should come back with the bearers to carry away the beast. The sooner it is skinned the better so that the fur can be preserved.

Here are the various steps a hunter should follow to obtain a good result on a tiger hunt:

- Wisely choose the region for the hunt
- Choose the proper site for a blind
- Build a good blind
- Select and place a bait
- Be quiet and cautious while waiting in the blind.

*Choosing the region for the hunt:* It is best to hunt in high-altitude terrain. Tiger fur is always thicker in cooler areas. My favorite regions were near the small village of Nam Banh, 30 kilometers (18 miles) from Da Lat, and Kong Pan, a village between Djiring and the plateau of Cagne. Those places had so many tigers in the fields that I always shot two or sometimes three in one month.

*The site for the blind:* Before deciding where to place a blind, be sure that tigers live in that region. The best way to do so is to explore the area some 10 to 20 kilometers (6 to 12 miles) around the village where you plan to set up your camp, especially the paths leading to rice fields or neighboring villages. Look for the sign left by the cats, such as paw prints or scratches around the places where they bury their droppings, or very old tracks littered with porcupines' needles.

Never forget that either old or new sign means tigers are in the region. Set the blind in the neighborhood of the trails, but far enough from them and in a secluded enough place (like a dense forest or a grove of bamboo) so that the animal can eat the bait quietly without being disturbed by villagers going to or from the fields. The tiger will stay in a region as long as it can find something to eat.

If the bait is small enough to be carried, the best site for a blind is a place in deep shade. However, if the bait is a gaur or an elephant killed in a forest clearing or out in a pasture, try to camouflage the blind as well as possible with branches and grass, and try to hide it from the vultures.

*Best type of blind:* Do not build the blind in a tree. The results are always negative—I know from personal experience. I finally adopted the system advised by Plas, an expert hunter, which was to build the blind on the ground. I added a few modifications to his design, and the result was productive.

I built the floor out of small branches of bamboo and the walls of bamboo, and covered the roof with *tranh* grass. The construction materials were gathered far from the site chosen for the blind. Cutting trees and bamboo nearby will trigger the quarry's suspicion—the tiger's senses are always alerted by any changes it perceives in its environment. The camouflage of the blind must be perfect, and must completely obscure the hunter. If the target animal looks through the shooting hole and sees something move inside, it will disappear and never come back.

*Tranh* is the grass used by the Montagnards to build their huts. They use it the way people in the European countryside use hay. Once the blind is built, cut an opening one meter (about three feet) square on the side facing the bait, and close it with a window made of *tranh*, which will be removed at nightfall in order to use the headlight. In that window should be a small "loophole" so that the tiger can be shot if it comes during the day. The area between the loophole and the bait should be clear. The blind should have the appearance of a natural bush. Place a man inside it, then go to the bait and observe whether you can see him. Block off any light that might illuminate the inside of the shelter. If nothing can be seen through the loophole from outside, the obscurity is perfect.

Noise and unnatural odors can be big problems, so avoid smoking, moving around, and snoring. The tiger will hear even a small noise from afar. That was the reason I always placed the bait twenty meters (sixty-five feet) away from the blind instead of the ten meters recommended by the old professionals. If possible, I wanted a creek between the blind and the bait; the running water would likely cover accidental noises made by the hunter.

*Selecting and placing a bait:* The best bait animal for attracting tigers is the sambar deer. An adult male or a big doe weighing up to 200 kilos (440 pounds) is ideal. A gaur or an elephant can also serve, and either will last longer than the deer. The only inconvenience is the smell of the gas caused by their putrefaction, for the bigger the body, the stronger the smell. In the beginning of my career I had to abandon a blind because the gas was suffocating me. After that experience I took into account the direction of the wind. Position the bait only after you construct the blind. It should be firmly attached to a big tree with unbreakable lianas (vines). Never forget that the tiger is incredibly strong. A good hunter must always try to foretell the unforeseeable.

*Precautions while occupying the blind:* My method of getting into the blind was simple: I asked my men to make a lot of noise when we arrived at the bait site. After making sure that tiger sign existed near the bait, I entered the camouflaged shelter, closed the door, and sprayed DDT powder on the floor to get rid of fleas, ants, and other insects. I spread my blanket on the ground and made sure I had within reach my Thermos of coffee, my gun, and my headlight in case I might have to shoot after dark. Then I gave the men the signal to leave, during which they made a lot of noise.

Tigers have the habit of staying in the neighborhood of a bait once they have started to eat it, so as to prevent another big cat, wild dogs, or boars from coming onto it. When people arrive, making a lot of noise, the animal will hide a little distance away, returning when it believes everyone has left. It may wait for thirty minutes or twenty hours before returning. Sometimes it starts eating immediately; other times it stares fixedly at the blind for a long moment without making a movement. If this happens, remain calm and motionless. If the cat hears the faintest noise, it will take off, never to come back. A hunter can shoot a tiger by day between seven o'clock and five in the afternoon, or after dark until around midnight.

My last recommendations to tiger hunters are these: Be sure your hunting area is not infested by "Sunday hunters," and do your absolute best to avoid wounding animals you intend to use as baits. Wounded animals may die later somewhere in the forest, and if a tiger finds a wounded animal, it will not go to your bait.

If you need to get meat for your camp, do not hunt near your bait, and preferably use a .22 Long Rifle or .22 Hornet, which makes less noise than a shotgun or larger rifle. For a hunt to have good results, you should place a bait and a blind at each point of a triangle five to eight kilometers (three to five miles) away from each other. The baits should be checked on the second day by a tracker you trust. Be patient while waiting for his daily reports—kill time by reading, fishing, or hunting small game far from the camp.

The wait in the blind is not easy. Not everyone can stay quiet and avoid drinking, eating, smoking, sleeping, or coughing for hours. Some hunters say that shooting a tiger in these conditions is not good sport. If they know of other, more productive ways, good for them. As for me, I found that my method was an excellent way to get a trophy by oneself, without having to buy it.

Shooting a tiger from a blind is not easy, either. I have seen a few hunters lose their calm completely when a tiger stared at the loophole behind which they stood. Some became so nervous that they missed their target from that short distance.

Tigers are rarely shot during unexpected encounters. Over my whole career I only killed three animals that way. The first time, I got *two*! It was the mating season, and I fell on a couple mating in the middle of the highway from Djiring to Da Lat in the light of a resplendent full moon. I put an end to their romance, miserable heartless hunter that I was! I encountered the third tiger and killed it during a night hunt for deer.

The vision of a tiger at the blind affected me in a way that is impossible to describe. I felt a mixture of fear, respect, admiration, and covetousness. It is simply a grand and unforgettable spectacle. I was usually alerted to the cat's imminent appearance by the breaking of a dry branch, the flying up of pheasants or wild chickens feeding on the worms of the bait, or the flight of a small wild cat or a boar. Other times I heard the cat's characteristic mewing as it approached the bait. Such signs place you on your guard and freeze you to complete immobility. After a moment you can see the animal feasting on the bait.

Sometimes nothing announces a tiger's coming. After looking at the bait hundreds of times without seeing anything, suddenly the hunter sees this ferocious animal glaring at the loophole. His heart skips a beat; believe me. Often the big cat stays motionless a few minutes, then comes to sniff the blind before going back to the bait. It will try to chase the flies buzzing over the rotten meat. It will growl, and perhaps try to move the bait to another place more to its liking. Its powerful efforts will shake the tree to which its prey is attached. When it realizes it cannot break the bait loose, it will start to eat with its eyes fixed on the loophole. The cracking of the bones it breaks between its powerful teeth is the signal I would wait for. When I had a client, I would try to calm him down and ask him to wait for my signal before shooting (most hunters made the mistake of firing too soon).

The first shot is very important. Seldom do you get the opportunity to shoot a second time, unless the hunter has a double rifle with two cartridges. I always advised a double-rifle hunter to load up with one softnose and one solid bullet, and to use the softnose when aiming at the heart and the solid bullet when aiming at the neck. If the tiger faced him, the target was the base of the neck.

After the shot, wait a little while. If everything seems quiet and you can see the tiger, check whether the tail is moving. If not, the animal is dead; otherwise, shoot a second time immediately. A tiger with a bullet in the heart still can run two hundred yards.

To avoid having to go after a wounded tiger, I always tried to shoot it in the neck with a solid bullet, which would almost surely break its cervical vertebrae and drop it right away. That shot was deadly on elephants, bovines, and big cats.

## Gaur

Montagnards using the *Koho* dialect call this animal *k'bay.* The Vietnamese call it *con minh*. It is the tallest bovine in the world. An adult male stands 1.8 meters to 2 meters (6 to 6½ feet) high at the withers and weighs up to 2,500 pounds. Its bulk makes it look terrifying, but it really is not. When I would see a herd of those formidable bovines in pastures early in the morning or at nightfall, they looked like peaceful domestic cows. Gaurs, like tigers, are now greatly reduced in Vietnam. Properly speaking, the gaur of Vietnam is an Indochinese gaur and is very slightly different from the gaur found in India and in Malaysia.

The skin of a gaur is dark black, the forehead and legs pale blond—it looks as if it is wearing gaiters. Its horns are very heavy at the base but not long considering this animal's size. The male's horns are more developed than those of the female, with the horns having a wider spread. They are black at the base, greenish-gray in the middle, and black at the points. The horns of the young are yellow in the middle.

The gaur has an impressive chest that seems to epitomize the animal's strength, and it is difficult to knock one down with the first shot. On its back is a good-size hump extending from the back of the neck to the middle of its body.

The gaur's ferocious look frightens beginning hunters, conjuring up visions of a diabolical monster. Its eyes always seem angry and bloodshot. At age fifteen, during my first encounter with a huge gaur, I imagined that it breathed fire from its muzzle while it charged me.

This tireless animal travels very long distances to reach its pastures. It likes uneven terrain, dense bamboo forests, and old Montagnard rice fields. It can be found in the pastures at dawn or late in the afternoon. In the rainy season it can be seen at any time. The pursuit of the gaur is especially difficult in mountainous regions.

In spite of its ferocious looks, the gaur is very shy. Its sharp senses of smell and hearing warn it of danger and it takes flight without hesitation. It never charges without a cause. The pain of an old wound can make this animal very dangerous. When wounded or cornered, it will first try to escape before charging to the death, which makes some hunters believe that it charges without provocation.

I once shot a huge bull near the small village of Ternum, twenty-five kilometers (fifteen miles) from Da Lat. It had charged five Montagnards, two men and three women returning from the fields with their baskets full of corn. Two of them escaped while the three others died with their bones smashed. Later this bull also killed two Vietnamese soldiers sent on its tracks by the local mayor, who asked me then to shoot the aggressive and dangerous animal. After a pursuit of three hours, during which the bull tried three times to escape without charging me, I shot it down. It was a magnificent bull measuring 2.17 meters (7 feet) at the withers. Its horns, very heavy and symmetrical, were a wonder, with a spread of 45 inches. Its weight? It appeared to be only hide and bones.

I discovered that it had been shot earlier, the first time in the jaw and another time in its left thigh. It had other, more recent wounds in the chest and belly. Hornets 5 centimeters (2 inches) long were entering its wounds and coming out with small chunks of decomposed flesh—they were eating the poor animal alive. It could not feed itself because of its broken jaws and pierced stomach, and was a walking corpse. It was easy to understand why it had become so aggressive, charging and killing people without provocation.

The gaur lives in herds of ten to twenty. The old solitary bulls stay in the neighborhood, awaiting a female in heat. The best regions to hunt them were the high plateau of Lang Bian between the Cam Ly River and the province of Fyan, and the plateaus of Djiring and Cagne.

Once a hunter was able to locate them in his hunting area, everything became easier. I would proceed methodically, depending on the season, searching for pastures in the region. By arriving in the pastures early in the morning or late in the afternoon, I could find the animals without having to cover great distances. During the rainy season the tracks are easy to follow. Even an amateur can do it. During the dry season they are less visible. Other problems hunters must deal with are the animals' sense of smell, which is more acute in the dry months than during the monsoon season, and their tendency to go to the swamps, where it is cooler.

Approaching a herd requires a lot of caution. The faintest noise or a change in wind direction can ruin a hunt. The most difficult approach is through forests because the animals usually smell you and get away. I do not recommend that method. I found it best to go to the pastures at dawn or nightfall. I used a good scope in the afternoons and solid bullets in big calibers such as the .404 Jeffery, .375 H&H, 9.3x64, or .458 Winchester. At short ranges I would aim at the neck to hit the cervical vertebrae. At long distances I would shoot at the chest or the shoulder one-fourth of the way up from the base of the chest.

For medium-size game I used an 8x60 Mauser, 7x57 Rigby, or .30-06 Springfield. To get meat for the camp I shot a .22 Long Rifle because it made far less noise than a shotgun (a 12-gauge would make a thundering noise and frighten away any nearby game).

## Banteng

This animal was often called *boeuf sauvage* (wild ox). Its Montagnard name was *k'rou* and its Vietnamese name *bo rung*. The hides of cows and the young are a light reddish-yellow with a white belly. Like the gaur, the banteng has "gaiters" (and foreheads) of a dirty blond color.

A large bull banteng will measure 1 meter 50 to 1 meter 70 (5 to 5½ feet) at the withers and weigh 800 kilos (1,750 pounds). Also like the gaur, it has a hump on its back, and similar, although less massive, horns that can spread 80 centimeters to 1.10 meters (31 to 43 inches) on a large bull.

When I hunted with Ngo Van Chi in the region of Dông Mé in the plain of Krong Pha, I killed a monster banteng that measured 2 meters (6½ feet) at the withers and weighed 900 kilos (nearly a ton) on the scales of the Dông-Me station. It had only one eye, but its horns spread 53 inches. My .404 carbine held horizontally passed easily between them. I gave my trophy to Charles Vally, a planter of Djiring and a well-known hunter of that period. I was not rich enough to have it registered. According to him, my trophy was six inches over the world record at that time, which had been shot in 1920 by Fernand Millet, an officer of the game department in South Vietnam.

Many of my trophies were of good size. I sold them or left them in the Montagnard villages for lack of bearers to carry them. I never considered getting animals that qualified for any record books, because in my opinion anyone can do that. An elephant big or small requires the same amount of preparation to shoot. The relative size of the tusks makes little practical difference. Since I was always in the jungle, it was normal that I got sometimes record-caliber trophies.

## Asian Water Buffalo

In the *Koho* dialect this animal is called *r'pou*, in Vietnamese *trâu rung*, and in French *buffle sauvage*. It is much bigger and more massive than the domestic buffalo commonly seen in the rice fields. It looks like the buffalo of India and has a massive and powerful neck. Its hide is black or dark gray, depending on its environment. Its horns are a beautiful shiny black. A large male stands 1.5 to 1.70 meters (about 5 feet) at the withers and easily weighs one ton. Its horns, although impressive, are not appreciated as trophies. They usually span from 1 meter to 1.8 meters (40 to 70 inches) between the points, which are needle-sharp at their ends.

The buffalo lives in herds of ten to fifty animals or by itself. People have talked about herds of two hundred in the plains of La Lagna and R'Pouma Klong. Personally I never saw anything of that kind. This bovine is also on the way of extinction due to repeated epizootic disease outbreaks in Indochina. I recommend shooting it with big-caliber solids. It is an ideal bait for the tiger.

# Why and How I Became a Professional Hunter

## Chapter 3

By the age of three I was already very interested in firearms. I would spend long hours in my father's office, where he kept his collection of guns in a magnificent cabinet made of rosewood and enclosed by a pane of glass. I admired with wide eyes the patina of the stocks in French or Circassian walnut, the blue-black metal of the barrels, and the silvery gray of the engraved breeches. They fascinated me.

Among those weapons were hunting guns and two small gallery rifles. They were a 9mm Buffalo, made by the famed French firm of St. Etienne, and a loose, old 9mm Flobert that clicked like castanets when someone touched it. With its huge hammer, the engraved trigger shield, and a few golden nails I had encrusted into its stock, it really looked like an old Arabian musket. For that reason, my uncle Robert, who was four years older than I, had named it the "Arabian gun." It was, frankly, ugly.

The French philosophers claim, however, that you can always discover a certain beauty in all ugliness. The following anecdote proved them right: When the Japanese occupied French Indochina on 9 March 1945, they issued a decree ordering all Frenchmen and Vietnamese, under penalty of death, to turn in their weapons, ammunition, cameras, and radio sets. The decree instructed that rifles, smooth-barreled guns, as well as all pistols and revolvers had to be surrendered. We obeyed like everyone else. We knew it was easy for the agents of the Kempetai, or Japanese military police, to find out which people had not deposited their weapons since all firearms had previously been registered at the French Surety. We did not want to risk being tortured or beheaded for trying to hide weapons.

After the defeat of Japan toward the end of World War II, the Kempetai gave back all our weapons. Nothing was missing, except my hideous "Arabian gun," which a Japanese soldier had perhaps found to his taste and had kept as a valuable addition to his arms collection—thus verifying the correctness of those old French philosophers' thought that all ugliness had its beauty.

When my father surprised me one day dreaming in front of his gun cabinet, he said, "You are impatient to go hunting and try your little carbines, aren't you? Wait two more years—when you are five, you'll go hunting snipe with me."

He was fanatic about hunting those birds. His promise only half pleased me. I really wanted to use all his firearms. "And the other carbines—when can I use them?" I asked[1].

Laughing, he pinched my round cheeks, pretended to look at his fingers, and replied, "You are still too young, *mon petit* (my little one). Look, I pinched your cheeks and milk is still coming out. When you have a mustache and a beard, you can use the other guns."

I almost screamed in my anger: "But you don't have a beard or a mustache, and you hunt with them!"

He ruffled my hair, which I always combed carefully, and replied, "Because I shave them."

Then, taking me in his big arms, he pulled my face against his, kissed my cheeks, and then rubbed mine against his to show me how scratchy they were. It felt like sandpaper.

A few months later he went on a trip to Saigon, the capital, and came back with a new gun. I was shooting arrows with my little pistol when he came into the room with a very small carbine at his shoulder. I believed it was even shorter than my Flobert. I felt immediately drawn to it, dazzled by its elegant shape. My sudden and irresistible attraction to it was like a thunderbolt—I could not take my eyes off that wonder. I was bewitched.

"Papa, is that for me, that little carbine? What is its make, its caliber? Please show me its ammunition."

[1]While those words might seem too sophisticated to come from the mouth of a three-year-old, they were quite natural to me since my parents never used baby talk with me. They always spoke to me as if I were much older.

I asked for his permission to hold it. I grabbed it with shaky hands, sniffing its metallic scent. My father explained, "It's a British carbine, a Martini-Henry, made in 1875. It was used in the war of the English against the Zulus and the Boers in Africa."

My eyes wide open in ecstasy, I asked him with a shaky voice, "Do you want to trade with me? I will give you both my carbines for your Martini." (At that early age, I was already using the proper terms to describe firearms because that is how my father always talked to me.)

When he saw how seriously I was speaking, he went to his suitcase and took out of it a magnificent belt full of copper cartridges that shone like Vietnamese red gold. They were sparkling and I thought they were winking at me. My father held out one of those bewitching cartridges.

"Look, Tiennot, it's a solid bullet. It's much smaller than the big 'bananas' I shot with my .404 Jeffery. Well, if you shoot at a gaur or an elephant with this bullet, you can kill it as surely as with my rifle. But there is a big problem—the recoil of this little Martini carbine is much stronger than even that of the .470 Express elephant gun."

I then remembered the blue-and-green bruise on his shoulder after a shooting session when he fired a total of ten cartridges with those heavy elephant guns. He was screaming in pain when my mother rubbed his injured shoulder with camphor alcohol. I was sixteen before I lost my fear of the recoil of a new carbine.

My apprenticeship as a hunter and shooter began when I was four. I was living then with my grandparents in a chalet on top of the mountain pass of Ro-Tong, near the sea city of Nha Trang in the south of Vietnam. My grandfather and my father had obtained a contract to build a road, a railroad, and a tunnel connecting that city to Ban Me Thuot in the high plateau. They had to finish the construction work in one year. My mother, who was pregnant, was living in Nha Trang with my little sister, Helene. My father had settled in a small straw hut on the beach, at the foot of the Ro-Tong Pass in order to be on the site of his work. I spent all my weekends up until Sunday afternoon with him.

I accompanied him when he went hunting wild chickens, francolin, and doves to replenish his food supply. Sometimes he brought back a big hare. I flushed the game, then put what he had killed into a large game bag slung across my shoulder. I gave its contents to the cook, who then prepared for us an excellent dinner, which always included a seafood soup followed by a salami of pigeon or rabbit. It was with my father that I spent the best moments of my young life on top of the "laterite mountains," as people called the red dirt of that region. During the weekdays I was restless like a caged rat, going aimlessly from one room to another.

My grandfather finally realized that I was bored. To distract me, he began to tell me the story of *The Last of the Mohicans*, the masterpiece by James Fenimore Cooper. Then he showed me the many other volumes on his bookshelves.

"*Mon petit*, you see these books? It is in one of them that I read the story of the Mohican. There are many other interesting stories. You'll know them too if you can learn to read."

He did not have to exert any pressure to make me a most attentive student. He taught me how to connect the letters of the alphabet, and in six months I was able to read fluently and understand everything I read. I started with *The Count of Monte Cristo* by Alexandre Dumas because the main character's name was Edmond, like my father's. In spite of my interest in the Count's adventures, however, I was not happy being inactive. I needed physical activities such as walking, hunting, or fishing. My grandfather, seeing my continuing restlessness, decided to replace the slingshot I used to hunt with a beautiful little gallery rifle, a Flobert with hammer and extra-long hexagonal barrel. That wonderful 6mm rifle was much more accurate than my 9mm carbines, which shot round bullets.

My grandfather decided to teach me to become a little marksman:

"Do exactly what I tell you, and in fifteen days you'll shoot as well as I do," he promised. I began to make cardboard targets measuring no bigger than four inches. He laughed when he saw them and said, "Your targets are too small, my little Genjo" (the name he called me sometimes). "Don't forget, you are just starting."

I insisted, however, on using them.

The lessons began. He showed me how to load and unload the rifle, how to aim with an open sight, and everything else I needed to know to become a sharpshooter. I followed to the letter all his explanations. After five days of practice I succeeded in placing all my bullets in the targets. I was bothered, however, by having to walk the twenty-five yards to the targets after each shot to check on the accuracy of my aim. After thinking seriously about this problem, I found a solution. I shaped white clay into small balls to use as targets. Once they were dry, they would explode with a white smoke when hit by my bullets. If only lightly brushed, the ball would drop to the ground, and my bullet would get lost in the air with a mewing sound. I was in heaven. I imagined myself fighting next to my heroes Gary Cooper or Tyrone Power in the famous Khyber Pass on the Afghanistan–Pakistan border, repelling waves of fanatical enemy warriors. The background music in those war movies was always the mewing of bullets, which was like the noise made by my ricochets.

When my grandfather saw how prudent I was and with what dexterity I handled my carbine, he gave me a box of cartridges and his permission to go hunting on the construction sites after the workers had gone home in the afternoon. Thus, I could hunt every day without running the risk of hurting anyone by accident. I brought back turtledoves for the family table, and giant blue and red lizards for the cook, who made a medicinal mixture with them for his personal use. He explained to my grandfather that it was a powerful aphrodisiac drug that allowed him to give many children to his wife. My grandfather laughed and replied, "Bep (cook), I believe that you have many good friends eager to help you in this matter."

I listened to him intently but could not make the connection between the lizards, the cook's numerous children, and his good friends. However, I did not ask my grandfather about this, because I was sure he would answer that I would understand everything with time.

My life during that year was monotonous—hunting turtledoves and lizards each afternoon, reading Indian stories each evening, and staying with my father in his straw hut on the beach during weekends. From time to time a sparrow hawk or a falcon would hover over the chicken coop looking for easy prey. I then imagined myself as "Hawk-Eye," standing guard over his tribe with his long carbine, and I would shoot at the birds of prey, sometimes making them lose some feathers.

When the construction work came to an end, I regretfully left my grandparents and their chalet on the red-dirt mountain and returned to the high plateau of Lang Bian, where my carbines were waiting for me. I was five years old now and had not forgotten my father's promise to take me hunting snipe with him when I reached that age.

He kept his promise, letting me accompany him on each of his hunts, armed with the 9mm Buffalo. He looked so handsome in his felt hat and boots—my hero, that giant—carrying his 16-gauge Robust shotgun, his belt loaded with cartridges of different colors. I looked at him with admiration and gratefulness when he handed me my ammunition, five little green Gevelot shells loaded with No. 8 shot. When he saw the birds walking toward us looking for food, he whispered, "Go ahead and shoot, but wait until the birds are no farther away than 10 meters (about 40 feet)."

For me, hitting snipe on the ground with bird shot was like child's play. I remembered the 6mm Bosquette, with which I easily could have shot that game from twice as far and more. Sometimes the bird flew off, and I would aim and tried to get it in flight. My father explained that I should shoot quickly from the hip like American cowboys. Since my gun did not have much power, I could not take the time to bring it to my shoulder because by then the fast-flying snipe would be out of reach. So I had to shoot by simply pointing the barrel toward the target. The new method did not bring good results at first, but finally the day came when I could reach my targets four times out of five.

This good period of my life, which I thought would be eternal, did not last long. Eight months after our return to Lang Bian my father died of a pernicious fever complicated by the malaria he had caught during construction of the steel bridge over the Song Lagna River. The foundations of the bridge had been regularly broken into pieces by the tumultuous currents that developed during the monsoon. My grandfather and my father, working very hard with teams of coolies, had finally been able to make the foundations solid enough to resist the formidable pressure of the currents and support the bridge. At the inauguration of that vital bridge, my grandfather noted in his speech that the construction had cost the lives of eight hundred men and two hundred horses. They all died from diseases or snake bites, or were snatched by tigers or the flood. My father was one of the casualties of that long and difficult engineering project.

The death of my hero left me intensely distressed. For a long time I cried each time I thought of him. And often when I went hunting snipe all by myself, my eyes were so full of tears that I could not see the birds flying off. It took me years to get past that tragic period of my life.

Every Sunday my uncle Robert and I went hunting together. I was older now and had a 32-gauge shotgun that I used with better results than my old 9mm Buffalo. For my eleventh birthday my mother gave me my father's 16-

gauge Robust. With that gun I began to hunt medium game like sambar and roe deer, and wild boars. Robert and I hunted by night with our Winchester 6-volt headlamps. Since there were not yet any precise hunting regulations, we did like all the other hunters of that period: We rode our bicycles to reach the hunting areas, and the Montagnards carried the game home on their backs over distances of fifteen to twenty-five kilometers (nine to fifteen miles). Back in the city, I gave a part of the venison to my mother, who had opened a restaurant. I sold the remaining meat to butchers, which allowed me to buy my clothes, batteries for my hunting lamps, and fresh ammunition.

I used my father's 16 Robust until the day my mother heard me say to Robert that I had fired two cartridges loaded with Brenneke slugs from a distance of thirty meters (one hundred feet) without killing the buffalo I was hunting. Fearing I could be hurt in the jungle with that insufficiently powerful gun, she decided to give me the carbine of my choice from my father's collection of firearms, especially now that I was sixteen and was the man of the family.

My mother, a widow without any pension, was not wealthy, and she had a hard time raising her little family of three children between the ages of twelve and sixteen. She worked very hard but could not give either my sisters or me the pocket money that all the French kids received from their parents for their small extra expenses. So at sixteen I could not go to the very popular dances organized by young people at that time—called surprise parties, or *surboums* or *surpattes*—because I could not pay for my contribution. I had also another important problem—I did not have the proper clothes for those events. I had only military fatigues and ugly big shoes called *Pataugas,* which made me look like a young homeless person compared to the other boys wearing elegant *gayabera* shirts, gabardine pants, and black suede shoes. The only way for me to correct that situation was to go hunting and sell my venison to the city butchers to get what I needed.

However, that sort of enterprise was not easy at that time—the second half of the 1940s, when the revolutionary movement led by Ho Chi Minh against the French was in full swing. The Vietnamese who joined his cause became guerrillas and took to the jungle. They were called Viet Minh, and were redoubtable. The Vietnamese sometimes referred to them as *con nai hai cang,* meaning deer with two legs because they lived in the forests. Hunting at that time was very dangerous, not only because of the risk of a bad encounter with wild animals but also because of the presence of the guerrillas. But I was sixteen and willing to take risks to get for myself all the pleasures a youth my age craved. I trusted my Montagnard friends to give me the best information about the moves of the Viet Minh, and I was full of confidence in my skill as a sharpshooter. Therefore, I decided to go hunting and sell the venison to the various city meat shops.

I had shot several times with a 9.3 Mauser and the .303 Winchester model 1895, but the cartridges were old and often misfired. So from my father's collection I chose my favorite weapon, the Martini-Henry. Its cartridges, too, were old and often misfired, but I found a solution—thanks to the presence of the French navy in Da Lat, where I lived. The cool climate of the mountain city was better suited than the heat of Saigon for the recovery of wounded or sick soldiers. So the French administration had opened a center there for convalescing fighters. The men of the garrison were still armed with antique 1892 Berthier carbines and 8mm Lebels with cartridges fresher than mine produced in the years 1939–1944 (my ammunition was made during 1928 to 1932). Their ammunition originated in the World War II years when French soldiers, still armed with those old weapons, attempted to oppose the invasion of the Germans, who had modern weapons.

I made a deal with the man in charge of the army food supply. He agreed to trade fresh ammunition for meat. He gave me ten packets of eight cartridges each, a total of eighty cartridges, for a swamp deer or a muntjac weighing about thirty kilos (sixty-six pounds). With the fresh cartridges I was no longer apprehensive about pursuing a wounded animal, so I decided to go after game more dangerous than sambar, muntjac, and wild boar. My uncle Robert, armed with the .303 Winchester, and I with my Martini-Henry took the train for the well-known Krong-Pha plain, where we could find herds of banteng—wild oxen less dangerous than the gaur. I shot a young bull that weighed seven hundred kilos (about fifteen hundred pounds). Full of confidence in my shooting ability and in the power of the Martini, I decided to confront the gaur (or *k'bay* in the Koho dialect spoken by my Montagnard trackers). What other animal deserved my attention more than the gaur, the beautiful trophy coveted by all hunters?

My first encounters with the *k'bay*, when I was fifteen, were not big affairs—I shot a few young bulls and females. Since I was never charged, I thought that gaur or banteng were no more a threat than big domestic bulls.

I soon learned that the Martini, a one-shot carbine, was not highly recommended for big-game hunting, so I traded rifles with military gunsmiths or simply with soldiers who owned firearms they had recovered during military operations. I exchanged a tiger skin, gaur or banteng horns, or a small pair of elephant tusks for some rifles (a .30-06 Springfield, a .303 Enfield, or an 8mm Mauser). All my military weapons were small calibers, which gave me some advantages. I could easily find fresh ammunition in metal packages, so I used the cartridges not only for hunting but also for frequent target practice. I soon acquired a well-deserved reputation among hunters for being a sharpshooter.

I believe I was born to be a hunter. I liked what I did, and I did it well. I could not imagine myself doing another job, especially one that put me behind a desk. I thrived on living in the immensity of nature, surrounded by simple people who shared my excitement in pursuing wild animals. Until I was twenty, I lived more often in the jungle than in the cities, earning more money than other men my age who worked for the administration or business companies.

When I inherited a good sum of money from my grandfather, I started a hunting company I named Sladang* Safari, which did not take long to become well known by local as well as foreign hunters. My clients came from France, Italy, and the United States. The most famous among them was Berry B. Brooks, a well-known American hunter. Soon I gained the reputation of being the best professional hunter and guide in Vietnam.

In September 1962 at the age of thirty-two, as mentioned in a previous chapter, I was expelled from Vietnam for reasons fabricated by the corrupt government of Ngo Dinh Diem. The expulsion put an end to my satisfying life as a professional hunter in the country of my birth. One year after my departure, the Diem regime was ended by a bloody coup.

*This is not a misspelling. In French Indochina, the animal known today as *seladang* was spelled *sladang*. For purposes of authenticity, the author has decided to keep the original spelling of his company throughout the text.

# My First Night Hunt
## Chapter 4

The only gun I had at this time was a 9mm Flobert. Later my mother gave me a 14mm Buffalo made by St. Etienne, a more serious although not ideal weapon—with it I got more feathers than birds. That little carbine did not have the necessary power to allow me to shoot francolin, wild chickens, and ring doves. I was frustrated and did not know how to convince my mother to let me use my father's 16-gauge, Robust. He had bequeathed all his arms to me, but I could not use them because of my young age, soon to be eleven.

Among the hunting guns with smooth barrels, I had the 16 Robust and a 12-gauge Verney Carron. I was not strongly built, and the recoil of these guns frightened me a little. I wanted to try the 16, but my mother remained unyielding. So I continued my hunts, without much enthusiasm, and kept on gathering only tufts of feathers, which I kept for my collection.

I was becoming a man, however. On my eleventh birthday my uncle George, my mother's brother, came to visit and gave me two gifts, a book, *Raboliot*, and a box of cartridges for my 14mm. He was surprised at the moderate joy I showed over the ammunition. Usually, cartridges were what I liked best. To hell with chocolate or building blocks—I wanted cartridges, only cartridges.

After a few minutes of conversation, my uncle understood my problem: "You are eleven today," he said. "I am going to ask your mother to let you come with me to the plantation, where we'll have your first night hunt. We will hunt *con nai* (deer)."

I replied sarcastically, "With what—my baby gun for pigeons?"

He started to laugh and explained, "I am going to take the opportunity of your birthday to talk to your mother and make her understand that it is time for you to have something more serious than these guns with a cork. I will suggest that she let you use your father's 16-gauge. Is that OK with you?"

Seeing the joy in my eyes, he continued, "Let's go and talk to your mother."

After a few arguments, she gave in but said to me, "Be very careful. If you kill someone, I am the one they will put in jail."

I reassured her, saying that I had never injured anyone with my 9mm or my 14mm. Why should I start to do so with a 16-gauge? Then, when I saw that she was already half convinced, I asked for her permission to get my gun in the "treasure room." I preferred to strike while the iron was hot, and do so in the supportive presence of my uncle. Later she might change her mind. I explained my haste by saying that the weapon needed a good cleaning since it had not been used for a long time.

She did not know that I had a key to that precious room and that I spent all my Sundays cleaning my father's guns. But when I discovered that all the 16-gauge shells were loaded with small shot and only a few contained buckshot or slugs, I was crushed.

My uncle reassured me, saying, "We are going to load cartridges for your hunt. Don't worry."

There was in that special room everything necessary to load rifle and shotgun ammunition. My uncle filled twenty cases with black powder and 00 buckshot, showed me the can of powder, and said, "It's the best." I believed him immediately. My knowledge of explosives was very limited. To me, black powder, T powder, and pyroxyle powder were all the same. They would explode and kill better than the 14mm. That was all I wanted.

After loading my cases, he filled the shells with melted wax. According to him, this would allow the shots to remain well grouped. He was the expert, and I listened to him with respect. I filled my cartridge belt with my new buckshot shells. Since there was still some room, I filled the remaining loops with five shells loaded with No. 6 shot for small game—I wanted to try my gun on wild chickens. We went to get batteries for my headlight, a Winchester that required five batteries. My uncle gave me a dozen (old Evereadies) and spare bulbs.

I put in my hunting bag the clothing and proper shoes for that first expedition. I did not forget my Marble hunting knife, its blade as sharp as a razor. After the birthday dinner celebrating my coming of age, I left with my uncle in his old Ford Model T truck. No need to say how happy and impatient I was.

We arrived two hours later at the plantation, and I received my first shooting lessons at night with a headlight. I aimed at the dog's eyes, which reflected the light, then at those of some cows in the stable. My uncle explained very clearly how to level and aim my gun at the animals' phosphorescent eyes, and how I had to lean my headlight at an angle that was convenient to me because I was left-handed. Before long I had learned the ropes. In my mind I became Raboliot, poaching at night with his dog Aïcha, my 16-gauge replacing the dog.

I could hardly sleep that night, so excited was I about the next day's hunt. I thought about it all night. Before closing my eyes I looked at my Robust, my hunting bag, my lamp, my knife, all of them neatly placed on the table. The patina of the gunstock shone in the candlelight before the flame slowly went out.

At dinner the next day we had wild chicken *à la citronelle* (lemongrass), products of my testing the new gun. I had tried my Robust, which had a thirty-inch-long barrel with modified and full choke, and was able to shoot accurately with it. I was thinking about the poor deer I would kill. We left after dinner, walking from the plantation to Mr. Mermouth's orchard five kilometers (three miles) down the road. He cultivated delicious Valencia oranges. I walked behind my uncle, who lit the road with a six-volt battery taken from a motorcycle. A young Montagnard boy my age followed us, carrying my spare batteries, a bottle of tea, and a flask of rum for my uncle, who believed that the drink was the ideal remedy to ward off the cold.

"You will see," he said. "After three or four hours of walking in the swamps, when you are seized by the cold, a drink of this *eau de vie* (water of life) and you will be another man ready for action."

Later I tried his advice and found out that instead of gulping down that ninety-proof *eau de vie* from a flask, it was better to swallow a can of condensed milk. The calories in the milk warmed you up much faster and would not temporarily affect the use of your legs or the accuracy of your aim.

At the orchard my uncle picked up a few oranges to quench our thirst. As we ate them he said, "This place is crowded with deer and muntjac. Load your gun with 00 buckshot, which has twelve pellets. Adjust your headlamp and go forward. The honor of the first shot is yours."

Excitedly I adjusted the beam of my headlight to the proper angle, placed the cartridge belt like a bandolier (over one shoulder and across the chest) because it was too large for my wasplike waist, and was ready. My uncle let me go alone for the first hundred meters before following with the young guide.

Although I was full of excitement, it bothered me that my uncle was far behind me and I was all by myself in the dark in the middle of the forest. I thought about a possible encounter with the "big cat with whiskers," and dragged my feet in the hope that my two companions would catch up. My uncle noticed it and asked me to walk faster, which I did reluctantly.

Suddenly I saw eyes shining at the border of the orchard 50 meters (165 feet) away. They were like four electric lamps shining in the dark. And they were moving—they went forward and backward, then stopped to fix me in a strange way. They did not seem to fear the beam of my headlight. On the contrary, they were attracted to it. I had the impression that they were coming toward me. I made a sign with my hand behind my back. My companions stopped. Again I adjusted the angle of my headlight. The beam became weaker for a few seconds, then returned to normal.

Those Eveready batteries made in Saigon were playing tricks on me. Suddenly the thought of the tiger flooded back into my mind. Perhaps two of them were stalking sambar deer. My imagination convinced me that I saw white whiskers. I panicked and rapidly backed up while continuing to look at those eyes fixed on me. My uncle asked why I was retreating.

"I believe there are two tiger over there—I am almost sure of it," I replied.

I really believed I had seen whiskers and body stripes. My uncle told me to turn off my light. Turning on his own headlight, he bravely walked toward the danger. How I admired my uncle at that moment! After a few steps forward, he leveled his gun. A red light pierced the dark, followed by two blasts. I heard the noise of animals galloping toward me.

My uncle yelled, "Shoot! Hurry, shoot!"

I quickly turned on my headlight and saw, about 30 feet in front of me, a sambar deer staggering on its legs, apparently wounded. Its eyes were shining as it walked toward me. I leveled my gun in a practiced gesture, aimed, and fired, pressing on both triggers at the same time. The results were a thunderous noise, a recoil that jolted my shoulder, and smoke as thick as a curtain of camouflage. Then silence. I reloaded quickly and jumped to one side to escape all the smoke released by the black powder, which screened the deer from my vision. I walked toward a rattling sound and saw a form lying on the ground. It was my deer, a doe. She was dead.

My uncle and I had done a good job. With two loads of buckshot I could not miss my target at that close range. I was proud. It was the first big game I had ever taken. My uncle asked whether I had hit my target. I showed him the beast.

"Good. We got two deer tonight," he commented.

He asked for his flask of rum and, while having a gulp, gave me instructions. I was to return to the plantation with the young guide, wake up the cook, and tell him to send an oxcart with two coolies to the orchard.

"Hurry," he said. And then he added with a laugh, "Look behind you from time to time, in case the young guide is caught by the tigers you saw."

His joke made him laugh, but when he saw my hesitation, he became irritated and warned me, "If you are scared, say so and we will go back to the plantation together. But don't count on me to take you hunting any longer."

We had planned to go to Krong Pha to hunt banteng the next day, and I did not want to miss such an opportunity. Now I answered confidently that I was not bothered by the dark but rather by my batteries, which were almost dead.

"Then walk in the dark," he replied, but he changed his mind and said, "Here, take my headlight and leave me yours."

I had no other choice but to obey him. I took my courage in both hands and, my guts tightened with fear, left with my guide. Of course, I knew that since he was behind me, he would be the first to be taken away by the tiger!

During that hike I repeatedly looked back with apprehension, afraid I might see the grimacing face of a big cat instead of the young boy. Finally dawn was coming. The wild roosters of the neighborhood started to celebrate even though the sun was still below the horizon. In the still blackness of night I saw a round red eye amid rows of carrots as we went through some vegetable gardens.

Intrigued, I approached and discerned two big ears. It was a hare having its breakfast. I shot it with a load of birdshot. It took some effort to get that cartridge out of my belt because I was shaking with excitement. After the blast, I waited a little for the smoke to dissipate. But I could not find my hare. I had missed it. I was not used to my uncle's headlight, which was too big and heavy for me. I felt disappointed for having missed the makings for a stew. As the sky became lighter, I told my guide to look for the hare on his return trip. I could not accept the idea of having missed the animal.

"Look for it everywhere in the rows of carrots," I insisted.

Finally we got home. I took my breakfast and went to bed after that eventful night. My tireless young guide went back with the cart and a companion. In bed I felt nauseated. I went to the bathroom to vomit. It happened two more times, along with headaches and stomach cramps. Finally, fatigue overcame my sickness and I sank into a deep sleep.

Three hours later my uncle woke me up. He held up a huge hare that must have weighed at least 3 kilos (6½ pounds). I had not missed it after all! I had wounded it and it had gone a little farther to die. Looking at me, Uncle George exclaimed, "What happened to you, Etienne? You are yellow like a lemon—your eyes too. Look at yourself in the mirror."

I explained the symptoms I had felt before going to bed. He said very seriously to me, "I hope that you are not down with an attack of malaria. It's not the best moment. Wait until after the wild bovine hunt to be sick."

Then he left, shaking the hare in his hand. As he went he said, laughing, "A good Burgundy hare stew will put you back on your feet in no time." The idea of the stew made me sick.

At noon I was still not on my feet. I felt very sick. Diarrhea caused me to go to the bathroom several times, the headaches and cramps had worsened, and my eyes had become alarmingly yellow. My urine was the color of very dark tea and my skin was lemon-yellow. My uncle panicked at seeing me in that condition and decided to send me back to my mother. Since his car was in the garage for a service, he walked me to the train station, bought a third-class ticket, and installed me in a rail car. Then he gave me a wad of banknotes.

"It's your share of the hunt, minus the price of the ticket. I sold the deer to the village butcher. I hope you won't be too sick. I am sure you are having an attack of malaria, but it's better to see the doctor. It might be something more serious."

He shook my hand and wished me a prompt recovery. "Take good care of yourself and come back soon. The bantengs will wait for us. I am going to a friend's to get a few slug cartridges for your 16. That way you, too, will be able to shoot. See you soon."

I spent three excruciating hours in that train compartment. We had to climb the Dran Pass, and the train progressed very slowly. I had to go to the bathroom several times. I vomited everything I swallowed, even liquid.

When I reached Da Lat station, I could not find a taxi and had to make do with a horse-cart, which took very long to get me home. I opened our door on shaky legs and holding my stomach. When my mother saw me, she rushed to support me.

"You are burning with fever, my little baby. I have to call the doctor right away!" she cried.

She sent one of her restaurant employees to the doctor with a note. As he raced off on his bicycle, my mother prepared a cup of tea with milk—my favorite drink. I was almost dehydrated and swallowed the delicious hot liquid quickly, only to vomit it immediately. My mother cleaned me with a little towel soaked with lavender cologne, dressed me in my pajamas, and put me in bed to wait for the doctor.

He arrived a little later. As soon as he was through examining me, he asked me all kinds of questions, then diagnosed a bilious fever complicated with an attack of malaria. Although I had taken quinine when I went to the forests, the doctor said I'd previously had these types of fever in my blood.

"You shall no longer go hunting!" my mother warned me. "That's it. It's your stupid uncle who has caused your sickness. I knew this was coming."

The doctor explained to her that my illness was not contracted recently—I had had malaria for two years. He cautioned her, "It's not a joke—this bilious fever is very dangerous. I gave him an intravenous injection of *quinobleu*, and here is the medicine your son should take. No solid food, only liquids such as tea, soup, and orange juice. I'll come back tomorrow morning to take his blood for analysis." He left with a preoccupied look.

I almost died. But thanks to the care of this good doctor I recovered. The attack of malaria was followed by a different and pernicious fever, the name of which I never knew. In some people's opinion it was a jaundice caused by deep fear. Others thought I had typhus. A few years later I came down with similar symptoms, and it turned out to be wood typhus. I did not become yellow, but I had violent headaches that made me want to beat my head against a wall, along with stomach cramps, diarrhea, and vomiting. Fortunately, a new "miracle" remedy had just come out on the market.

As far as the jaundice was concerned, I believe today that the intense fear I had felt when imagining the yellow eyes and white whiskers of a tiger during that hunting trip triggered the attack, especially since I was already infected with malaria.

My mother eventually sent me to my grandparents in Nha Trang to recover. I traveled alone by train. During the trip I stared out the window, waiting impatiently for the train to cross the Da Nhim River on the big steel bridge—the work of my father a few years earlier. I was in a hurry also to see again the entrance of the Mermouth orchard, where I had killed my first sambar deer on my first night hunt. Much later I often thought about all this with pleasure and could not help thanking my uncle in my heart, which I did by saying a short prayer for him. He had been the only one to understand my passion for hunting. He had taken the initiative to obtain my first serious gun from my mother. And he was the one who had taken me on my first night hunt.

He died from tuberculosis. I found him one morning lying on the floor of his room, eyes turned upward and his face covered with blood. He had in his hand the book he was reading, *Un amour de Swann*, a novel by Marcel Proust.

# The Solitary Gaur of Riong Tho

## Chapter 5

At the age of fifteen I hunted with my father's little Martini-Henry and his leather belt that was always full of shiny cartridges. I had been in love with that gun ever since I first saw it as a three-year-old. It became my obsession, my passion, and finally it became mine.

I decided to go after the mean and impressive gaur, known as seladang or *k'bay*. I left home on my bicycle and headed for the Montagnard village of Nam Banh, where my friends K'Sou and K'War were living. It was twenty-five kilometers (fifteen miles) from my house. In my hunting bag I had enough food for five days, spare clothing, and my carbine.

In the past I had often seen herds of the huge *k'bay* in the pastures, but too far away to shoot at, even with my heavy shotgun slugs. This time it would be different. I had the British Martini-Henry modified to take the 8mm French Lebel rifle ammo, much more powerful than the slugs, so I could now meet one of those monsters on equal terms. A solitary bull should not be confused with a young bull or a female.

I could not find my friends at their village. K'War, my guide and hunting companion, had gone on a fishing expedition with his brother K'Sou and a group of Montagnards. His wife told me he would not be back before the next day. I could not wait for him since I had only five days left out of the ten-day vacation for Christmas, so I decided to go hunting with K'Loi, their father. The old man accepted my offer, but hesitated when I told him what kind of game I had in mind.

He examined my Martini with contempt, spat on the ground, and, taking it from my hand, said with pity, "Ông Tienne [Mr. Tienne], this carbine is too small, its barrel too short, and the bullet too light for a 3,000-pound bull."

I pointed at my belt of shiny gold cartridges and explained, "This little carbine with this small cartridge can kill a gaur, even an elephant."

He listened but did not seem convinced. I gave him a few buckshot shells and four slugs. He and his sons used a Belgian 12-gauge shotgun with external hammers, a loose old weapon that made noise like a rattlesnake when one touched it, but it shot accurately. K'Loi had received it in 1930 as a gift from an old hunter of the neighborhood who was well known for his famous book, *Les Grands Animaux Sauvages de l'Annam (The Large Wild Beasts of Annam)*. Upon the old hunter's departure for France, he had offered K'Loi his gun as a souvenir. K'Loi was proud to have been the hunting guide of that great hunter, Fernand Millet, and constantly had Millet's name in his mouth when he talked about his past hunts.

For a long time K'Loi looked at the four fat black shotgun shells, German Brenneke slugs, I had given him. In his opinion, they seemed more efficient than the J.R. or helix shells he was using. These were pointed and consequently would pierce better. Finally he put them into a little pouch made of braided reeds that he wore around his neck when he hunted.

He started to give me a briefing on how to hunt the *k'bay* (gaur), and he could not seem to stop. He had hunted the ferocious animal with Papa Millet. The beast was fearless, he said, and charged without hesitation. We would have to do what Millet had done—wait for it without wavering and, when it was ten or fifteen meters (about thirty feet) from us, shoot it between the eyes. He had never seen Millet flee, and he expected as much from me.

He started to annoy me with his constant references to Millet. He said to me, "You know, Ông Tienne, I am old now and I can no longer run. My old legs will not allow it. And as for climbing a tree, it's out of the question."

I knew he did not know how to climb a tree. I always liked to joke with my guides, so, very seriously, I asked him, "K'Loi, if the gaur runs away, where should I put my bullet?"

He thought deeply about this dilemma, but could not find a satisfactory answer for me. Finally he realized I was joking. He pointed at me with an old finger deformed by arthritis and, laughing, said, "Ông Tienne, you are always joking. Wait until you see Mister *K'bay*—then you won't laugh anymore!"

K'Loi woke me up very early the next day, and we had breakfast together. He had soup made of fermented rice with two pieces of dried buffalo meat as hard as leather. I ate a large piece of toast on which I spread lightly salted butter and drank a cup of hot chocolate. We were now ready for action.

K'Loi and I took the trail leading to the Riong Tho village about ten kilometers (six miles) away. We had two bearers with us. After some distance, we saw the footprints a very large bull had made during the night. This place was not far from Fyan village, where there were *dâtches* (swamps of salty dirt that attracted many wild animals). It was still early, and K'Loi believed we could find our gaur in the pastures on the hills of Fyan.

We started following the footprints, which sank deeply into the clay of the trail. According to K'Loi and the bearers, the gaur was very big. We walked silently, avoiding the dead branches and leaves littering our way. My guide stopped after a while and showed me a pile of fresh droppings. He dipped his toes into that mash, then said with a smile, "The animal is not far. We'll be on it soon."

Excitement made me perspire abundantly, and my hands became sticky. I tightly squeezed the Martini and focused all my attention on the tracks. I did not want to lose them.

K'Loi led the way, holding his old gun. I followed with the other two Montagnards. We walked in single file, silent as shadows, even though swarms of gnats were harassing our group.

It wasn't long before I smelled the characteristic scent of bovines, a sweet mixture of stable and the pleasant odor of the grease that makes the gaur's hide shine. I again checked my carbine, loaded with a solid. K'Loi cocked his shotgun and we walked forward, careful not to make any noise.

In front of us the land sloped upward, covered with dwarf bamboo. The bushes were not higher than five feet, so we could tell that the gaur was not there. K'Loi went to check on the tracks while I crouched to better examine a huge footprint. The gaur must have eaten a few bamboo tufts before leaving that place. I was concentrating on those fresh signs when I felt warm breath smelling almost like chlorophyll on the nape of my neck. At the same time I heard a hollow cough. The gaur had silently gotten up from his bed and now towered over me. He had not seen me yet, however—I was crouched at his feet, staring, petrified, at him. His eyes seemed to have been injected with blood. He breathed through his muzzle with the noise of a forge. I could not help thinking that his breath had the good smell of freshly cut grass.

When he saw me, he took one step forward, then snorted. I thought I saw flames coming out of his dilated nostrils. I was paralyzed. The Martini in my shaky hands felt as if it weighed a ton. The monster seemed to unfold to his full colossal size, looming at least 6½ feet tall at the withers. All this happened in a few seconds.

Realizing how dangerous my position was, I threw my rifle at his head and fled down the little slope. He gave a powerful, hollow growl and charged me. I seemed to have wings—I was literally flying. What was chasing me was not a gaur but Lucifer himself, growling like a tiger, bellowing like a mad bull.

At full speed I ran toward K'Loi, who, gun in hand, waited for me to shoot. When he saw me without my weapon, pursued by the monster that seemed to spit flames, he disappeared, as did the other two guides. The gaur had before him a desperate flight of two-legged creatures and could not make up his mind which one to pursue.

While running for my life, I found a bent tree that I could climb easily and rapidly. I scrambled up to a height of three meters (ten feet), which put me above the danger and allowed me to watch the scene. The gaur stopped and smelled the air with his smoking nostrils, apparently intrigued by my sudden disappearance and the flight of the other bipeds.

He decided to go after K'Loi, who had lost his loincloth. His turban, too, became unfolded and floated along behind him. He was like the great French king Henry IV, who was known for the distinctive white feather he wore on his cap when he went to war. The king was quoted as saying to his soldiers, "Follow my white feather." Here, it was K'Loi's white turban that attracted the attention of his pursuer.

During the chase K'Loi had dropped his gun, his cartridge bag, his tobacco, and his shirt. He wore only the unfolded turban, which seemed to fascinate the gaur the way a toreador's red *muleta* fascinates a bull in the arena. My guide was lucky enough to find a pine tree sticky with resin.

The trunk was straight, without a branch up to a height of five meters (sixteen feet). He squeezed that unexpected luck in a passionate embrace and in no time was near the top of the tree.

I could not help being convulsed with laughter when I saw his face full of fear, his eyes wide and looking everywhere, his disheveled long hair sticking to his sweat-shiny face—and above all his lack of clothing. He was naked as a worm, squeezing the sticky trunk with his arms and legs and now looking at the monstrous madness below him.

The gaur turned back after losing K'Loi, though he kept spitting and panting with anger and pawing the ground with his hoofs, furious at having lost his victim. He scrutinized the horizon with myopic eyes, impatiently searching for that biped. I could see the Martini shining in the sun in front of him. The rifle seemed to reproach me for having dropped it. I wished I could hold it at that moment.

After a few more bursts of anger, the gaur left, maintaining a martial bearing. He fascinated me. With his shiny black hide, dirty blond gaiters with a tuft of the same color on his forehead, he was magnificent—the image of strength. His perfectly symmetrical horns must have spread more than forty-four inches between their widest points. He looked back several times, then trotted away—to my great despair. I had missed the opportunity to shoot a very handsome lone bull.

My guides and I waited for a while before coming down from our trees. Soon we heard voices coming from the wood. It was a group of Montagnards going to or coming from a fishing trip. K'War was among them. He saw us, his father and me, in our embarrassing situation. Spotting the Martini, he picked it up and gave it to me. I could not help feeling ashamed. He guessed what had happened and told us they had seen that magnificent gaur walking 50 meters (165 feet) from their group. The beast kept looking behind it as if expecting to see someone on its trail.

One of the bearers handed K'Loi his clothing and the gun he had lost in the escape. Millet's great tracker did not look proud of himself, and did not say a word. K'War advised us to return to the village, since it was too late to follow the tracks of an alarmed animal that was already on its guard. We decided to resume the pursuit the next day.

That evening after dinner, K'Loi offered the traditional jar of fermented rice wine. After several drinks he started to reproach me for my lack of self-control. Because of my flight, we had lost a trophy the likes of which no one in the village had ever seen, even though there were many gaurs in the area. I replied that it was my first encounter with such a monster, and that the bull must certainly have been a bad spirit spitting fire like a dragon—K'Loi himself had seen flames coming out of the enraged monster's nostrils. I was the subject of their jokes for a few minutes. Then I asked for their attention and began to speak.

"You know, K'Loi, I was very afraid for you today. I thought you could not run and did not know how to climb trees. What I saw confirmed that you can run faster than a gaur and that you climb trees better than a monkey."

All K'Loi's guests and family members burst out laughing—so hard that they had tears in their eyes. K'Loi laughed more heartily than anyone else. Good old K'Loi! After the feast I asked him whether he would accompany K'War and me later, since it was already three in the morning. He stammered a vague excuse—he had to go to Da Lat to sell a few pigs. I understood, however, that he had lost his confidence in me and my skill as a hunter.

Fortunately, Ông Bà, the good spirits of the forest, granted me revenge on the huge gaur of Riong Tho. I saw him again. He was taking a bath in a muddy pond in the woods, making so much noise snorting in the water that he did not hear my approach. I was shaking with excitement. My guide's face became taut—I could sense his fear. The sight of that massive animal disturbing the pond, and the noises it made breathing and spitting water through its muzzle, revealed a power that made us feel vulnerable. About thirty meters (one hundred feet) from the beast, I aimed and put a solid into its huge neck, breaking its cervical vertebrae.

Like a harpooned whale, the black mass emerged in a spray of muddy water, exhaled a sad bellow, and fell back into the pond, dead. I panicked when he got up after my shot, but decided to wait for the charge—without realizing I had not reloaded my gun!

I stayed there a long time admiring that wonder of nature, amazed that the animal that had scared me so much with its diabolical appearance and behavior now lay dead at my feet. Tears were flowing from his already opaque eyes. What had this prince of the woods seen at the moment of his last big jump into eternity? He looked sad and harmless now. Maybe his last thoughts and visions had been of the young cow for which he had followed the herd for some days. Or maybe the large pastures in which he liked to run. Or the fields of red rice and corn that smelled so good. Overcome with remorse and sadness before that creature I had just destroyed, I caressed the tuft of hair on his forehead and asked him for forgiveness for having ended his life.

To celebrate the success of my hunt, I offered the jar of friendship to my companions. K'Loi was back and participated in the drinking. He raised his hand to request silence and made a speech that I would never forget:

"Ông Tienne, you deserve this *k'bay*. This trophy, I would not have liked anyone else but you to shoot it. You dared to face the monster with that little single-shot carbine. Mr. Millet had a two-barrel elephant gun with cartridges as big as bananas."

The double-barrel Express .577 and .600 Jumbo had just made their appearance in Indochina. Every Indochinese hunter, especially the amateurs who knew nothing about guns, decided these doubles were the ideal weapons for big game. They would say, "The bigger the cartridge, the more powerful the rifle. The more leaves there are on the open sight, the farther away the bullet can kill the game." Those heavy and expensive guns had very little accuracy, especially at longer ranges, and were made for heavy and powerful men able to stand the tremendous recoil. They were ideal guns, yes, but only for amateurs loaded with money.

All the village had a banquet the next day. I took two legs and the fillets—600 kilos (1,320 pounds) of meat—which were carried to Da Lat on the backs of fifteen men. I had them delivered to the army steward with whom I had a contract for venison.

The horns measured 1.15 meters (45 inches) between the widest points, almost certainly a record, though I could not prove it, because the recording process was too expensive for my pocket. And anyway, I was hunting for a living and also for pleasure, but not for glory.

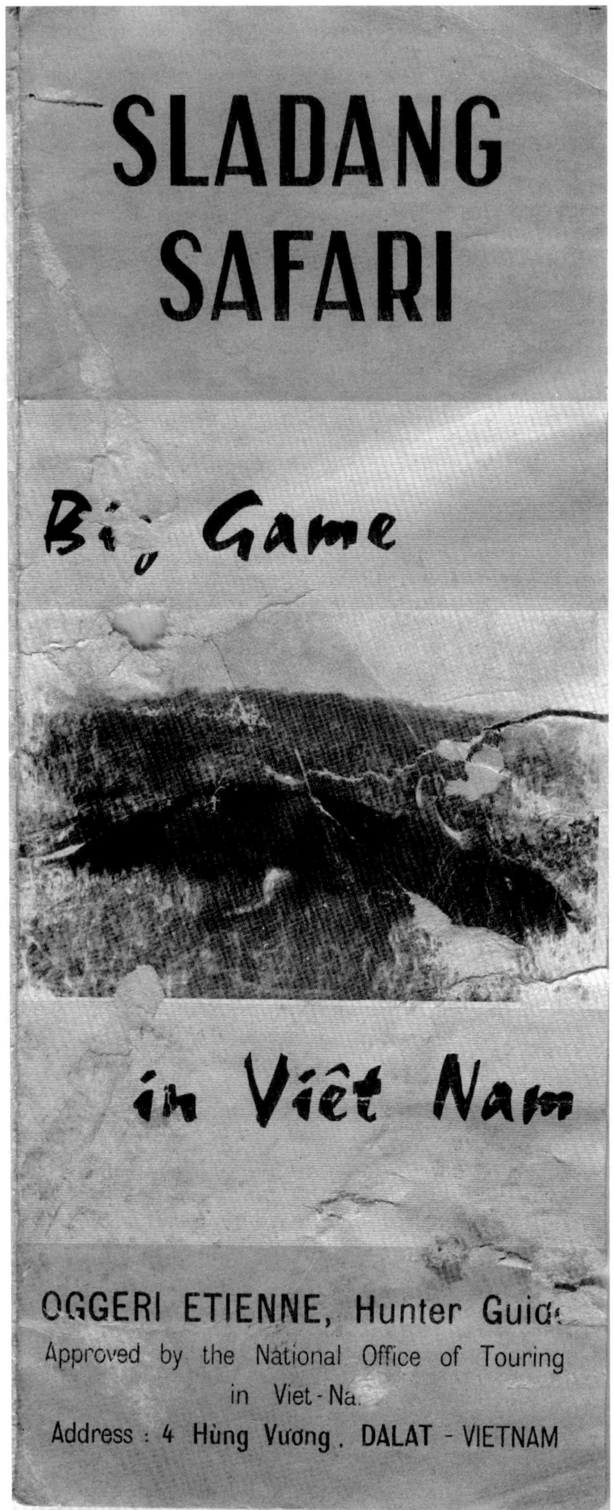

SLADANG
SAFARI
Bi Game
in Viêt Nam
OGGERI ETIENNE, Hunter Guid
Approved by the National Office of Touring
in Viet-Na
Address : 4 Hùng Vương . DALAT - VIETNAM


Sladang *is not a misspelling. In French Indochina, the animal known today as seladang was spelled sladang.*

## CONDITIONS

*A minimum of 15 days is necessary for the Hunter who wishes to see and shoot : 1 tiger ~~and 1 bovid (either Gaur - Banteng or Buffalo).~~ From ~~20~~ to ~~25~~ days for 1 tiger - 1 of the bovids and 1 elephant.* 25 to 30

## COST

### SAFARI "A" :

*SAFARI ~~of~~ from 15 to 25 days :* 100

Per day and per person : ~~80~~ US dollars or ~~5.880 piastres Vietnamese~~ currency.

Per day and for two persons : ~~140~~ US do[illegible] or ~~10.290 piastres Vietnamese~~ currency. 180

Per day and per person, either woman or man ac[illegible] panying the Hunter-customer : ~~40~~ US dollars. 60 [illegible]

NB. We never accept more than two Hunter-custome[illegible] at one time.

## MATERIAL AND EQUIPM[illegible]

*We supply the customers of our SAFARIS with :*

- The [illegible] from Saigon to DALAT by air.
- Jeep Land-Rover [illegible] for transportation of our customers to the hunt[illegible] area[illegible].
- [illegible]noes, fixed bamboo camps, or canvas tents depending upon the area.
- Coolies — Trackers — Boys — Cooks.
- Bedding : field-beds, sheets, blankets, mosquito-nets.
- Camping mat[illegible]ial : lights, radio receiver.
- Provisi[illegible] [illegible] lunch, dinner, five o'clock tea.
- [illegible] [illegible]lcool is left at the customers [illegible]
- [illegible] trophies,

The customers must bring nothing with them [illegible] their guns and ammunitions, personal clothes [illegible] whisky.

*WEAPONS : For BIG Game in Vietnam and for [illegible] to 25 da[illegible] [illegible]RI, we advise our cu[illegible]ers [illegible] bring wit[illegible]*

- One 378 [illegible] 375 [illegible] 5[illegible] and 2[illegible]
- [illegible] 300 Weatherby carbine or the 30-06 Winchester with 50 cartridges Soft Nose for the felines, the deer, the boar.
- One Shot Gun caliber 12 or 16 with 50 cartridges. (Peacock, Pheasant, Partridge, etc. . .)

*CLOTHING : It is necessary to carry for 15 to 25 days in the forest :*

- 4 kaki outfits ( trousers and shirts )
- 2 shorts and shirts
- 4 pairs of wool stockings
- 2 pairs of shoes with high leggings, or boots (this item is of the utmost importance, they are left to the customer's choice ).
- 1 sweater.
- 1 raincoat
- 2 pyjamas – 1 Safari Hat

## LICENCES

**A) Weapon licence.**
**B) Hunting licence.**

A. – Temporary importation of guns and ammunition for hunting in Vietnam.

Hunting tourist going to Vietnam and wishing to bring with them their guns must send a request for a licence to the Department of Interior of the Vietnamese Government, at SAIGON. They will be authorized to bring with them three guns – Or : 2 guns with rifled barrels
I shot Gun
with 50 cartridges for each gun

In order to allow the Department of Interior to deliver the requested licence in due time, the tourists should send that request altogether with the request for a licence from the Representative of Vietnam in their Country. In the request there should be mentioned clearly : the family name, first name, age, residence, occupation, length of stay, and the caracteristics of the weapon ( Trade mark, caliber, number). Two photographs 4x6 should also be attached ( 2 photographs and one request for each gun. )

On entering Vietnam besides the foresaid authorization given by the Department Interior, they should deposit at the Customs' Office 75% of the cost of the guns imported as bail-money. If the customer should wish to avoid making that deposit, we could answer for him with the Customs Officer. Notwith-standing, the bail-money will be refunded on their leaving Vietnam.

On leaving Vietnam the tourists must bring their guns back with them.

B. — Hunting licence CLASSE "A"

The hunting licence CLASSE "A" is delivered in SAIGON by the Department of the Waters and Forests of Vietnam.

68 US$

The cost of that licence is 4.800 piastres Vietnamese currency. It gives the hunter the right to shoot during the hunting season, that is from the 15 th September to the 15 th April : throughout the year for tourists

- one buck-elephant
- two gaurs
- two bantengs
- two buffalos
- four bears
- six deers

*The complementary taxes for the killing are :*

| | | |
|---|---|---|
| — Elephant | : | 10.000 piastres |
| — Gaur | : | 6.000 .. |
| — Banteng | : | 3.000 .. |
| — Buffalo | : | 3.000 .. |
| — Bear | : | 2.000 .. |
| — Deer | : | 2.000 .. |
| — Tiger | : | 2.000 .. |

Any request for a hunting licence should be accompanied with two photographs and a signed declaration.

## ADVICE

*It is necessary for the customers that wish to go on a SAFARI in Vietnam to send their requests for licences two months in advance, (hunting licence, gun licence, passport, visa) to let us know one or two months in advance :*

a – the exact date of their arrival in to Vietnam, SAIGON, where we will meet them.

b – the number of days they wish to spend in the forest.

c – the number of customers, taking part in the SAFARI : hunting-customers and customers accompanying the hunter.

d – what kind of game they wish to see and shoot.

The cost of a hotel room in SAIGON is at the expense of the customer.

After confirmation of the order for a SAFARI, we beg the customer to pay, 20 days before their arrival : 30 % of the total cost of the SAFARI, and the rest upon their arrival into Vietnam. The payment should be made by way of Traveller's checks. If for some reason, for which our customer would be responsible, the SAFARI should be conceled, the 30 % already paid would be kept by us.

## IMPORTANT WARNING

We state for the benefit of our customers that we cannot garantee that they will see and shoot the tiger.

As far as bovids and elephants are concerned, the success of the SAFARI depends intirely on our customers, on whether they are sportsmen and trained walkers or not (1) The game areas near car-trails do not exist any more in Vietnam.

(1) *to see and shoot a buck-elephant or one of the bovids (gaur or banteng) the hunter must walk sometimes 6 or 7 hours a day, and cover 10 or 20 kilometers over rough country.*

## SAFARI "B":

We organize that SAFARI class "B" for local customers that cannot afford more than from two to five days.

The hunting licence, the killing taxes are at the costomer's expense and we take a 7.000 piastres premium for each animal seen and killed.

Cost per person and per day : 3.500 piastres.

Cost for two persons and per day : 6.000 piastres.

We supply all the necessary material, personal and victuals.

We cannot garantee anything to our customers for that kind of SAFARI, except that we will do our best.

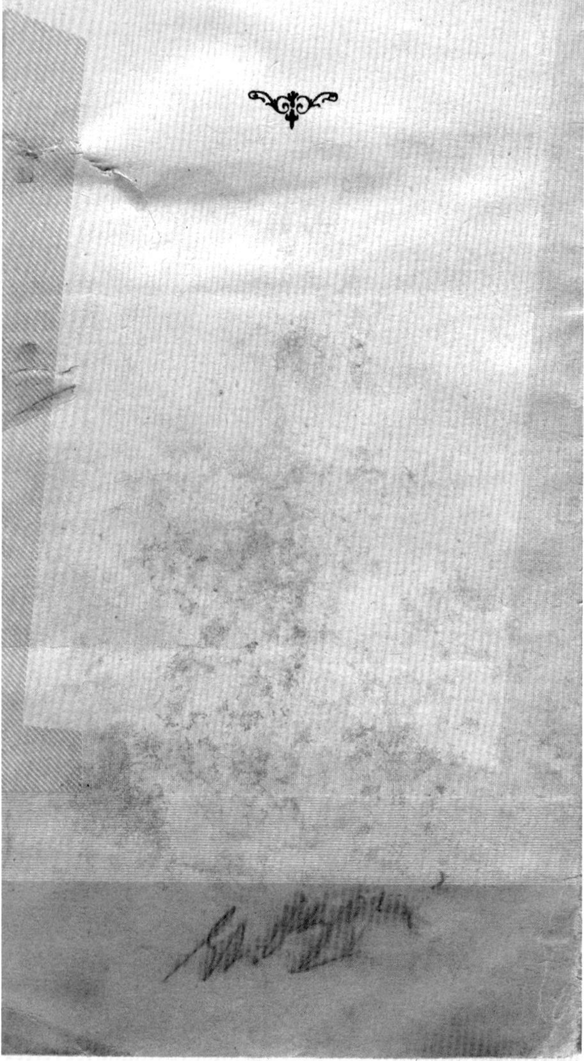

*The author shot this huge tiger with his Winchester 70 in .22 Hornet, placing a solid bullet under the left eye. The encounter took place at night and from a distance of sixty feet. Dông Mé, 1953.*

*Transporting six hundred pounds of venison to use as tiger bait on the plains of Krong Pha.*

*Near the Song Pha River, 1954.*

*Mother Nature's answer to the modern Jacuzzi—and a boon to tired hunters. Krong Pha, 1954.*

*Young panther killed on a night encounter in Dông Mé. Krong Pha, 1960.*

*Berry B. Brooks took this gaur while hunting with the author's company, Sladang Safari. Kinda, Bross Deur, Vietnam, 1961.*

B.B. Brooks returning to the camp with gaur. Bross Deur, 1961.

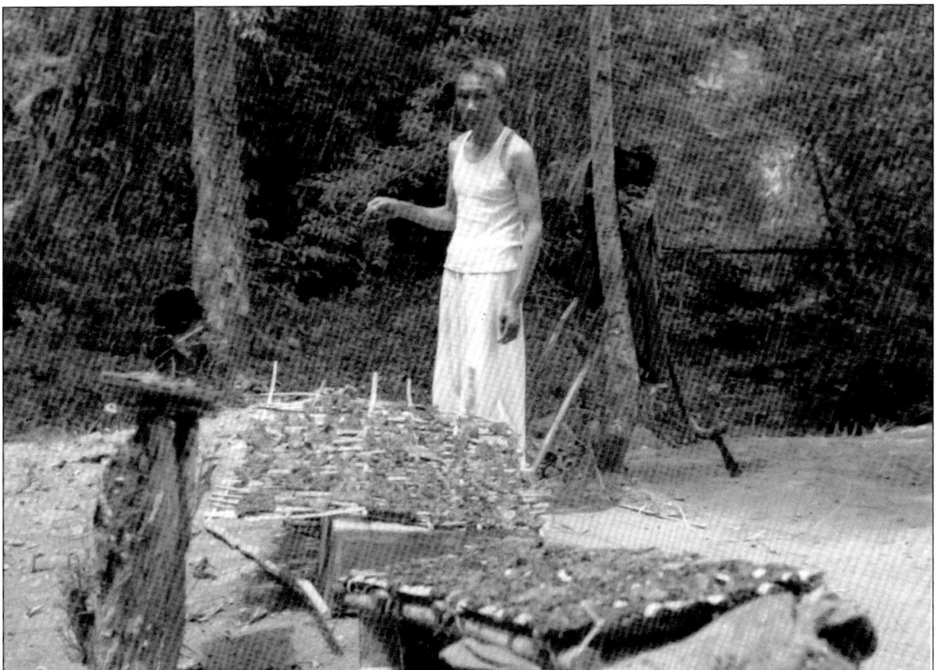

One of the chefs preparing gaur pemmican. Bross Deur, 1961.

*A nice doublet of panthers shot by the author's guide, K'Lai, on a night hunt in Krong Pha. Manoï, 1954.*

*Author's friend, La Quy Dac, and his first gaur, shot with a .300 Weatherby in Krong Pha. Manoï, 1954.*

*Golden panther shot by W. Consley, an American client of Sladang Safari, in Kinda. Bross Deur, 1961.*

*Young gaur shot by a client of Sladang Safari. Daglè Plain, Djiring, 1961.*

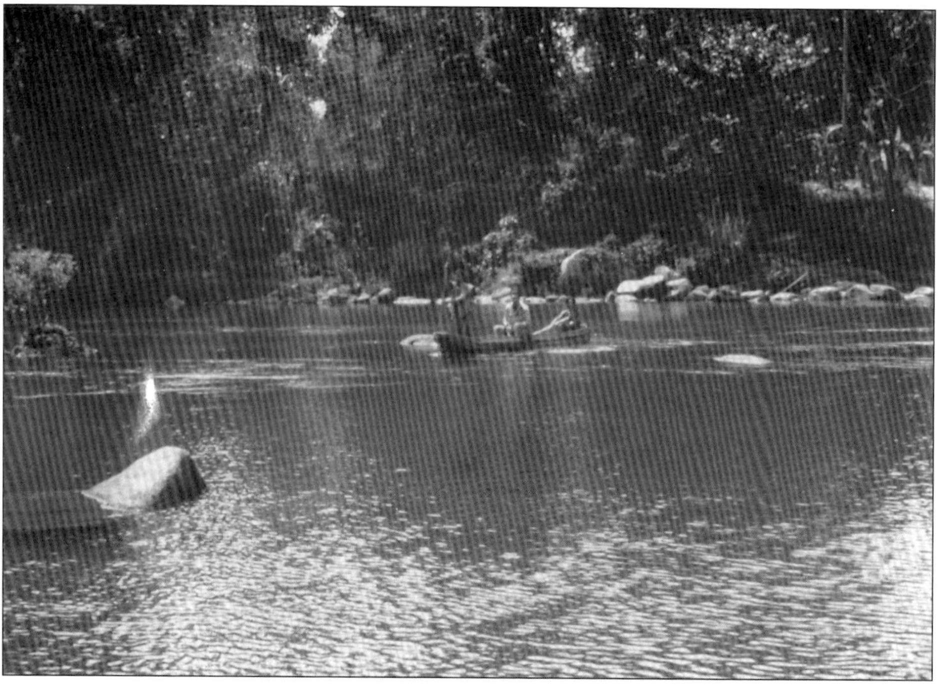

*The author crossing the Da Dung River to visit his blinds in Kinda. Bross Deur, 1960.*

*A young banteng shot by the author while trying out the first .300 Magnum Weatherby in South Vietnam. Manoï, 1953.*

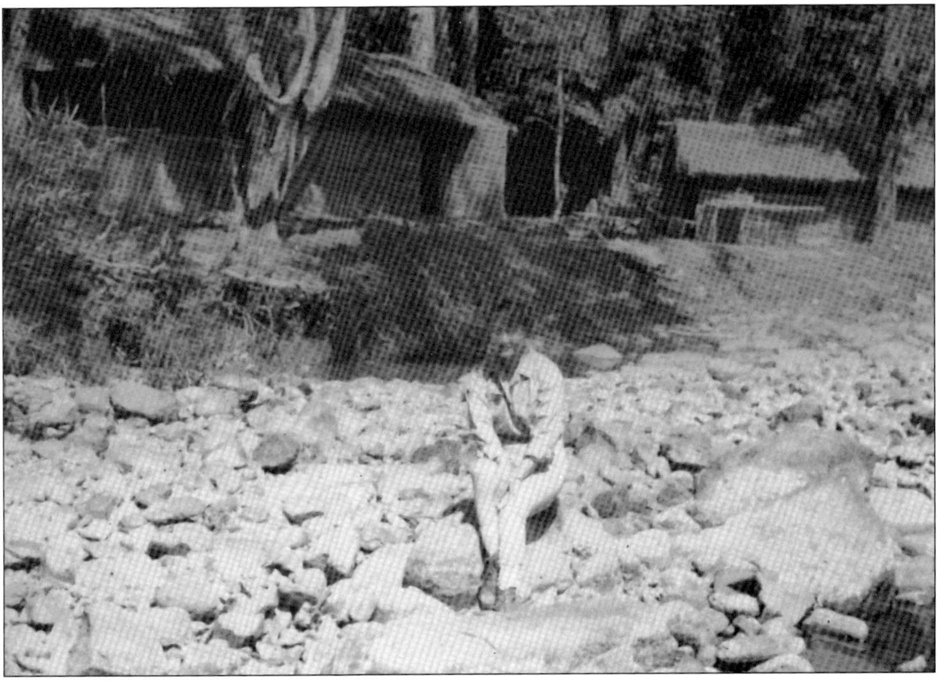

*Lechi at Sladang Safari's camp. Bross Deur, 1960.*

*The author with a gaur shot by his friend La Quy Dac. Manoï, Krong Pha, 1954.*

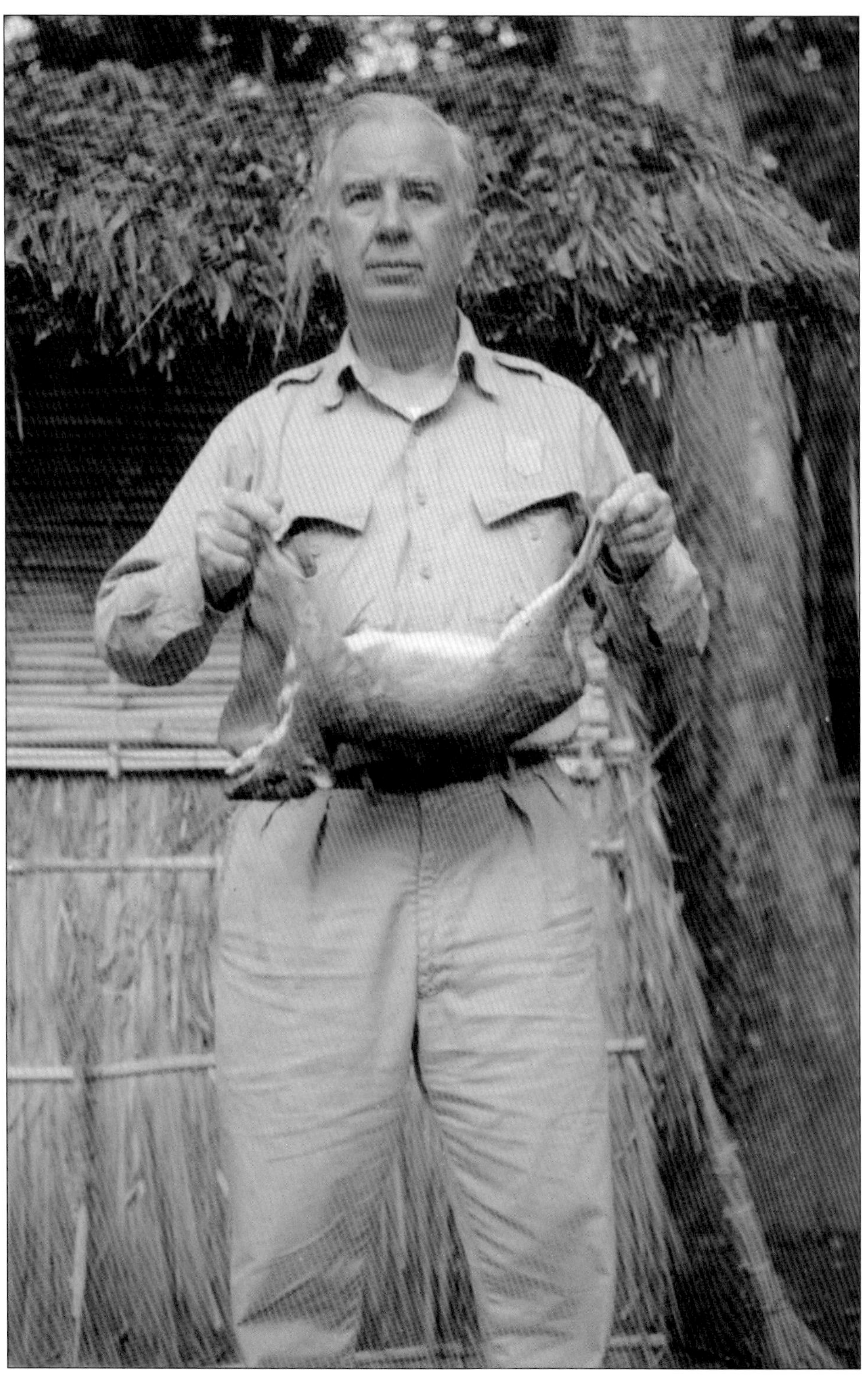

*Berry B. Brooks's first trophy was a mouse deer or* tragule *(the smallest species of deer in Vietnam). Kinda, Bross Deur, 1961.*

*Lechi with her second trophy shot with the author's .375 H&H Francotte on her first hunt with him. Nam Banh, 1960.*

*Lechi painted this picture of the author with his huge Asiatic buffalo shot in the R'Pouma Klong region in 1953.*

*Lechi painted this picture of the author with a nice trophy shot by Berry B. Brooks during his safari in 1961.*

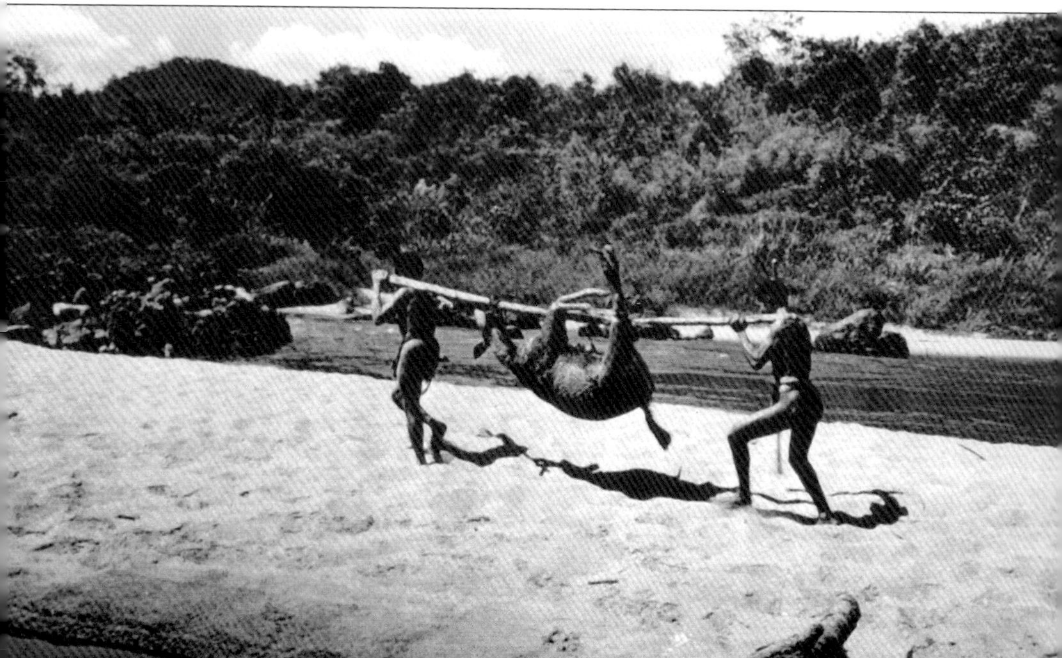

*Transporting bait for a tiger. Kinda, 1958.*

*Another picture of the author by Lechi, this time with his magnificent gaur (46½ inches between the widest points of the horns). Ternum, 1958.*

*Young tiger shot on a night encounter in Fya Nam Banh, 1948.*

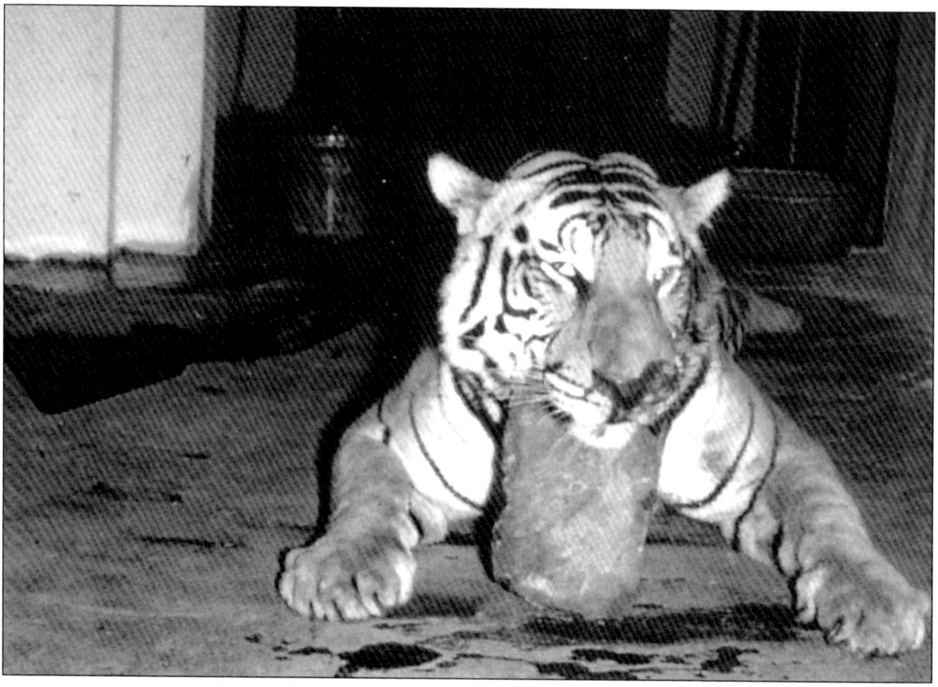

*The end of the cattle killer of Pleiku, 1950.*

*The sacrificial ceremony of a buffalo. Bross Deur, 1949.*

*D'Jarai village. Pleiku, 1951.*

*D'Jarai tomb, 1951.*

*Leaving for a hunt on elephant back. Bross Deur, 1952.*

D'Jarai girl getting water at the river. Pleiku, 1950.

D'Jarai girl weaving. Pleiku, 1950.

*The tusks of the record elephant (6 feet, 8 inches and 130 pounds) shot by the author in R'Pouma Klong. Shown in author's trophy room in North Carolina, 1992.*

*Back to the camp after shooting the tiger. Da Dung River, Bross Deur, 1960.*

*This record gaur had an inside-the-horns measurement of 44 inches and an outside spread of 50 inches. At that time, the world-record Indochinese gaur, shot in 1927, was recorded as having a 45-inch outside spread, so the gaur in this picture was a monster. Ternum, 1959.*

*B'Nar woman at her village water hole. Pleiku, 1953.*

*A big tiger shot by Lechi. Nam Banh, 1960.*

*Elephant with 44-pound tusks shot by a friend. Pleiku, 1953.*

*This Ma woman and child wear necklaces made from dogs' teeth. Kinda, Djiring, 1959.*

*This happy fellow with a weapon is a Montagnard from Kinda. Djiring, Vietnam, 1959.*

*An old D'Jarai man with a nice jar of alcohol. Djiring, 1950.*

*Author's friend Henri Portier drinking from a jar. Pleiku, 1950.*

*K'Loi was the best tracker in Lang Bian. Nam Banh, 1953.*

*Corn and rice silos, Vietnamese style. Pleiku, 1957.*

*A young Montagnard man from Pleï Hawen. Ankhé region, 1958.*

*The author shot this big tiger in Cagne. Djiring, 1949.*

*D'Jarai houses. Pleiku, 1958.*

*Author with a few skulls of sambar deer shot for the meat to supply orphanages and schools. Manoï, 1952.*

*A D'Jarai woman with bamboo earrings encrusted in enlarged ear lobes. Pleiku, 1958.*

*The Marquis de Monestrol with two nice trophies. Phan Tiet, 1968.*

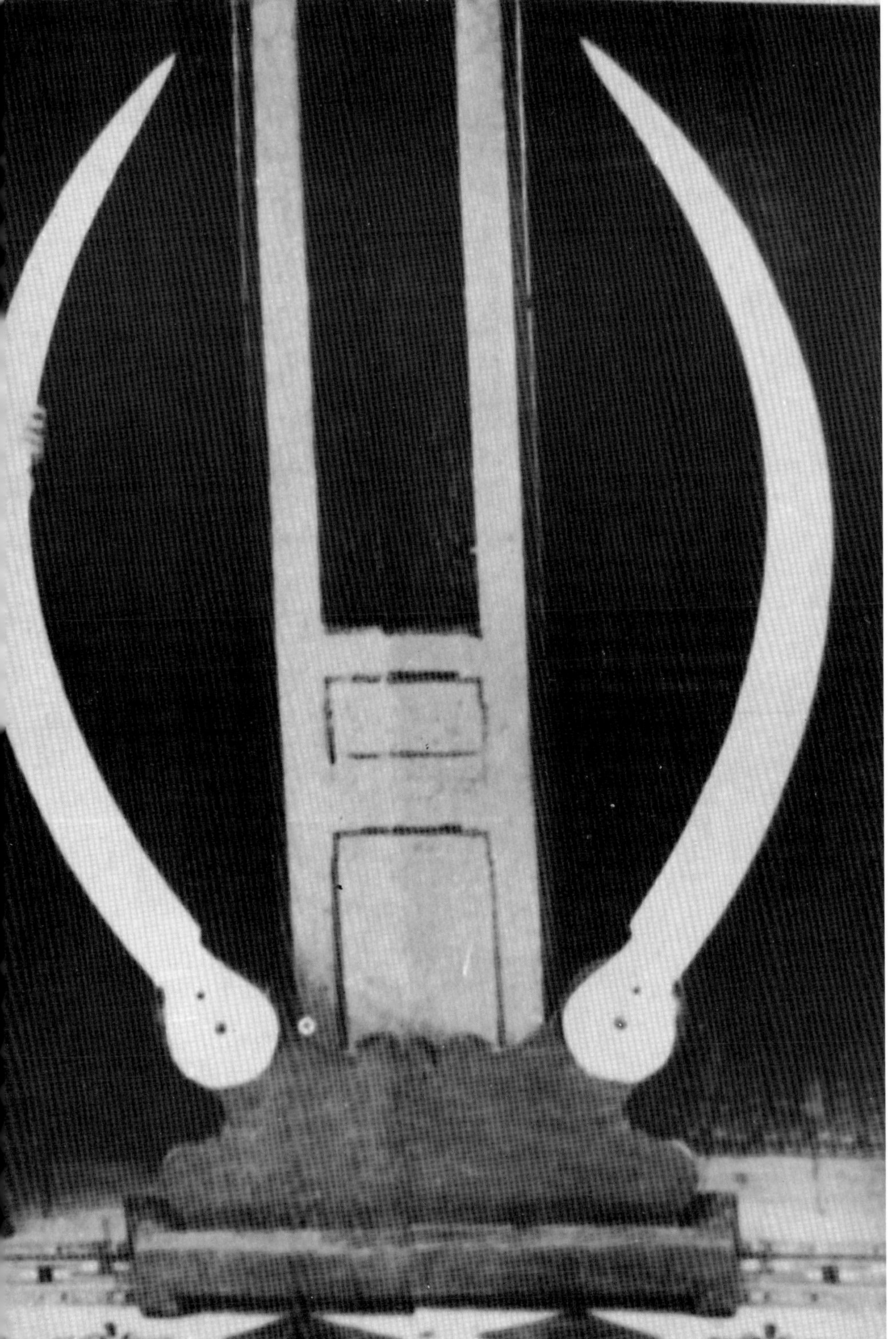

*The maestro and his copper gong. Nam Banh, 1946.*

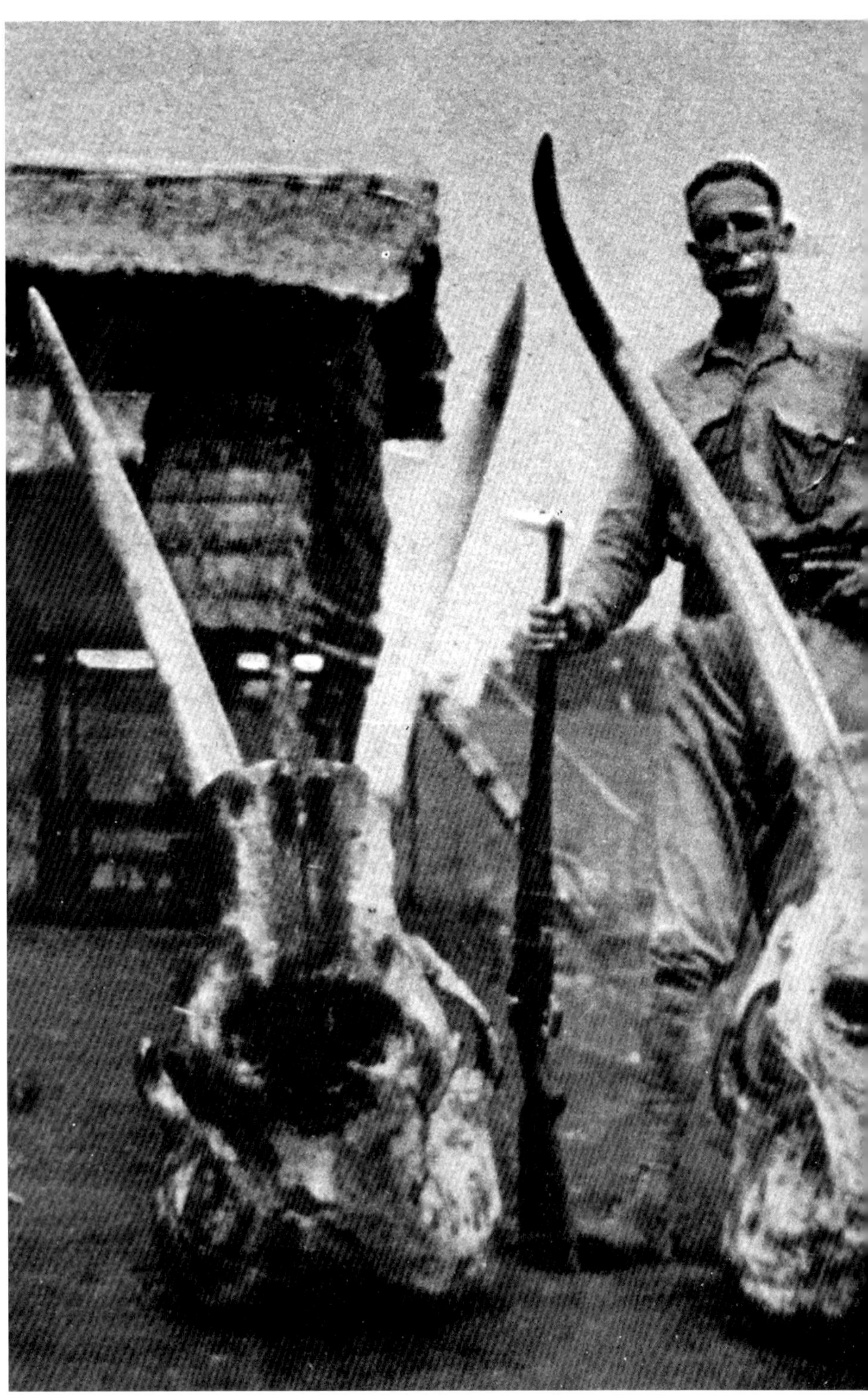

*Professional hunter A. Plas took these three nice elephants in twenty days. Kinda, 1937.*

(Photo courtesy of Aimé Plas, son of the professional hunter)

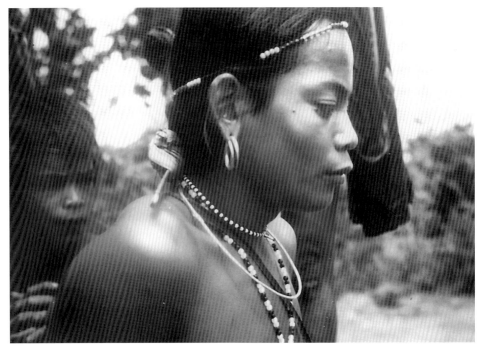

A Banhar woman. Pleiku, 1959.

Georges Rochelle, the author's friend, at a drinking party. Djiring, 1957.

# Stalking Tigers: My First Fiasco

## Chapter 6

I had set up my camp in Ternum, a quinquina (alcoholic bitters) testing station about twenty kilometers (twelve miles) from Da Lat. That area contained a group of small Montagnard villages, including Nam Banh, Bon Gia, and Riong Tho. Only one trail good enough for the passage of military trucks led from the army base in Da Lat to Ternum. During the French–Viet Minh War in the years 1945–1954, the military command garrisoned in Da Lat decided to regroup those three villages so as to have a base of operations in the middle of the jungle in case of an emergency action against the guerrillas. The French general in charge of the region believed that this system would prevent the Viet Minh from getting supplies and help from isolated villages. When regrouped and armed, the villagers would not be easily forced by the guerrillas to help them. To protect the area, the army had even given each Montagnard man in the villages an 8x57 Mauser rifle and ammunition. As was to be expected, the Viet Minh continued to get the rice they wanted, and the Mauser cartridges served only to wound a lot of wild animals.

The village in which my guide, K'Loi, lived was a part of Ternum.

My hunting companion, Jean Da Cruz, was with me. At that time we were two novices who had no experience hunting tiger. Neither he nor I had ever had any contact with the big cats. All we knew was a little bit of theory gleaned here and there from hunting books written mostly by amateurs. Fortunately for me, I acquired my little bit of knowledge about this very difficult quarry by reading the book *Les Grandes Chasses en Indochine (Big Game Hunting in Indochina)* by A. Plas, hunter and professional guide in Djiring, South Vietnam from 1930 to 1945.

I remembered a few important things, but not enough to ensure our success. That first hunt was a memorable fiasco. I needed at least two deer for bait. Jean, who did not like hunting at night, remained in the camp. I left with K'Loi, the father of my young guides, K'War and K'Sou.

We decided to go to Nam-Banh to shoot my bait, passing through beautiful forest clearings, large pastures, and old rice fields frequented by deer and sometimes gaurs. I was armed with an 8x60 Mauser, a semi-automatic .30-06 Garand (a rifle used by the U.S. Army in the Pacific during World War II), and a 12-gauge Robust with a rifled barrel that would take slugs or could be used with bird shot to take snipe at short ranges. That kind of barrel was like a sprinkler: When I used buckshot, the pellets would frame the target but seldom hit it.

We were wading in swamps and rice fields when I saw the first pair of eyes in the beam of my headlight. Their greenish color told me it was a sambar deer. While walking toward it I mentally repeated Plas's advice: "Shoot only to kill! No wounded beasts to escape to die in some ravine. Tigers would feed on them." I got within a good shooting distance of the deer, aimed five centimeters (two inches) under the eyes, and fired. The sambar fell with a bullet in its neck. We continued our hunt and I shot a big doe.

Since I had the baits I needed, we returned to the camp. On the way I saw several muntjac and swamp deer but left them alone. I had planned to kill a gaur to supply the village with meat. We reached the banks of the Cam Ly River between Ternum and Nam-Banh. The river was not deep there, but the current was violent. We had to hold hands, my men and I, to cross the torrent. I walked behind K'Loi, who advanced with the help of a stick. As we made our way across, I distinguished several pairs of eyes in the beams of my lamp. The space between the eyes was wider than that of a deer. I stopped K'Loi and pointed out to him the eyes. On the other side of the river was a *dâtches* (salt lick). He immediately said, "Shoot, Ông Tienne, shoot! These are gaurs coming to the *dâtches*!"

The animals were behind tall grass and I could not see their bodies. However, I recognized the bovines' characteristic smell of tallow. Since the village needed meat, I decided to shoot.

K'Loi crouched in the water as I aimed at the first pair of eyes. When I fired, the herd galloped off with a rumbling that dominated the noise of a nearby waterfall. Again I fired, three or four times, at some animals that had stopped to wait for their young ones. In a hurry to see the result of my shots, I crossed the river in a few bounds. Right away I saw my first victim, a huge domestic buffalo. Farther away lay two cows. K'Loi, who was behind me, screamed in despair and threw himself on one of the buffaloes.

"These are my buffaloes, Ông Tienne—you have killed my buffaloes!"

He became hysterical, touching the bodies of the animals and crying as if they were his wife or children. I tried to calm him down and handed him my flask of cognac. He took a long gulp, then explained that sometimes his buffaloes, kept in Ternum, wandered back to their former village and stayed there for a few days. I felt really sorry for K'Loi and asked him, "How can you recognize your buffaloes?"

He replied, logically, "And how can you recognize your black dogs among other black ones?"

He stopped crying when I promised to compensate him for the loss of his animals. But I would have to keep one as a bait for the tiger. I planned to set a bait near the salty place. I would have to kill at least two tigers to pay for the costly buffaloes. The big bull had fallen at just the right place for us to build a blind at the Cam Ly River. To limit the expenses, I sent a few men to Da Lat to deliver the two deer to the army. The sergeant major in charge of the food supply gave them a demijohn of ten liters of Algerian red wine with the admonition, "This is a gift for Mr. Etienne. You no drink."

I gave K'Loi the money from the sale of the deer. After drinking the wine and eating the roasted meat of his buffaloes, the old man said he was satisfied with the amount of money I had given him.

I trusted K'War and K'Sou with the building of the blind. I had chosen the place for it, a spot where one could often see tiger footprints on the path. Once the bait was well attached to a tree, I left the two young men to finish the blind. They knew how to camouflage it with bamboo and *tranh* grass. I went back to my camp to hunt snipe with my friend Da Cruz. We still had enough wine left to cook a few good dishes. One of the pleasures of hunting was good food enhanced by a good bottle of wine.

After finishing their work on the blind, my two guides came to camp to get the shotgun to take along when they went to check the bait every morning. This was my first mistake: Never give a guide a gun when he visits the bait, unless you are sure he will not fire on a tiger if he encounters one. I was sure my guides knew not to do that.

After his third visit to the bait, K'War hurried back to the camp and announced that the *k'liou* (tiger) had taken its first bites early that morning. The meat was still red and bleeding. K'War was very excited and told me that the animal must be colossal—he had never seen footprints so big. I believed him and we got ready to leave with a few coolies. My friend Da Cruz had been after a solitary gaur since five o'clock that morning, taking with him his 1892 Berthier and my .30-06 Garand that I had loaned him, since we did not trust the French Berthier ammunition (too many cartridges misfired). So I took my 12-gauge shotgun and my 8x60 Mauser with me. With Kynoch or DWM ammunition I could shoot big animals from the elephant to the muntjac. That rifle was remarkably accurate.

When we arrived at the blind, I went to see the bait and noticed that the footprints, clear and sharp in the clay of the *dâtches*, were indeed impressive—the size of a dinner plate. *That tiger must weigh 300 kilos!* (600 pounds at least), I thought to myself. Inside the blind, however, I saw that there was too much light. My men had skimped on the camouflage material, and beams of light passed through the roof and sides of the blind. I was furious and let K'War know about my irritation. To top off the disaster, there was no floor. They had made a little bench and put small branches on the ground. Since the blind was on a slope, the bench leaned to one side and was not stable. My guides had also forgotten to create a narrow aiming window. Instead they had made a large opening measuring 70x40 centimeters (27x16 inches).

It was too late to repair these mistakes. The shotgun loaded with slugs and my 8x60 with softnose bullets stood in a corner of the blind, within my reach. Night was falling, so I got inside the blind. I was still furious when I told K'War to leave with the coolies. I would stay by myself in the blind. I hung the headlight around my neck and attached the battery box to my belt. After drinking some hot coffee, I gave the men the signal to make a lot of noise, singing and talking, as they left. They were supposed to stop two kilometers (1¼ miles) down the trail and wait for my first shot before coming back to me. My second mistake, I realized as I settled in, was presuming that my guides knew how to build a blind, and my third was failing to check their work myself after they had finished.

Night was falling rapidly. The noise of some waterfalls 500 meters (a quarter-mile) away kept me from hearing well when, in the half-darkness, I saw a big form jump onto the bait and try to take it elsewhere. I aimed, but in the dark of the blind I could not see the sight. And there was still too much natural light outside to use my headlight. I saw the monster cat try several times to snatch the bait away. Fortunately the liana vines were solid. That tiger was colossal! It jumped on the bait, pulling it from side to side. I thought my first tiger would be a record trophy. When I heard the liana and the tree trunk break under the repeated attacks, I turned on my headlight and aimed. For a split-second I saw the tiger almost standing on its hind legs and dragging the buffalo by the neck. It saw the beam, let out a terrifying growl, and fled. Almost frozen by surprise and emotion, I waited a moment, hoping the animal would come back. But apparently it was as scared as I because it never came back.

The next day I had the rope strengthened and the blind repaired to make it more comfortable and functional, and decided to wait for the next visitor. The buffalo was almost intact—the monster cat had eaten only one leg. Two days later I shot at a beautiful tiger on the same bait, but missed! My Mauser had a double trigger, and in my excitement and inexperience I forgot how sensitive that system was and fired by accident. My second tiger, like the first one, did not return to the bait.

People sometimes say, "Never two without three." That was the case for me. After three days of hunting, my friend Da Cruz had to go back to the city. I was alone in my camp, thinking about that saying, when some Montagnards returning from Nam-Banh, where they had gone to pick up vegetables, told me they had seen a tiger in the *dâtches*.

It was two in the afternoon, and I was ready to go for it. I took my gun and my headlight, a Thermos of coffee, some raisins, and a bar of chocolate—food that I could chew silently. I got into the blind, and K'War and the four coolies walked away making a lot of noise.

After twenty minutes, quiet settled in and the tiger came out of its hiding place not far from the blind. It was a young male—not as impressive as my first two visitors, but I wanted a tiger, young or old. It was my first trial and I wanted to succeed. I took my time, breathing slowly to calm myself down. For ten long minutes I watched it snack on the already well-decomposed meat. Then I fired, my bullet striking the neck. It made a big jump, let out a rattling noise from its throat, and dropped to the ground. I jumped out of my blind like a little devil toy from its box (another mistake), and went to admire my trophy. I should have waited to be certain the animal was dead and to reload my gun. God, however, protects the innocent, especially if they are stupid.

That evening, while enjoying a rabbit stew with Algerian wine, I realized that if I were more experienced I would have bagged three tigers in one week! Later, the villages of Ternum, Nam-Banh, and Riong-Tho became my favorite hunting grounds. I paid my trackers well in money and game, and in periods of famine I gave them rice. When another hunter came to the villages, he never found guides or bearers. My men wanted to save the game for me.

That region between Ternum and Fyan was a paradise for tigers and gaurs. I never understood why the gaurs of Ternum were always by themselves. I never saw herds in that region, whereas in Nam-Banh, Riong Tho, and Fyan, which were only a few kilometers away, one could see many herds of bovines.

After my hunts I looked for a good book on big-game hunting. It was then that I made the acquaintance of Plas, the son of a professional hunter. I also met the Marquis de Monestrol and Charles Vally. All were great hunters who mentored me in my new vocation. However, in all honesty, I believe I owe my hunting success to the years I spent with my childhood friends, K'War and K'Sou, when we had as our mentor good old K'Loi, the greatest tracker on the high plateau of Lang Bian.

# A Tragic Hunt

## Chapter 7

My friend from childhood, François Da Cruz, decided to go hunting ducks with his older brother José, his sister Cécile, and her husband Paul on the first day of Tet 1950, the Vietnamese New Year. It fell on a weekend, and it was customary for people living in Saigon to go in search of waterfowl on these holidays. Their favorite hunting place was the rice fields of Cu Chi, not far from the city.

These fields had a bad reputation because the Viet Minh guerrillas were very active there. The Sunday hunters, however, did not hesitate to go there because they felt protected by the area's few French military posts, manned by two noncommissioned officers and about fifteen soldiers—Vietnamese, Algerians, Tunisians, and Cambodians. A command post of the Foreign Legion on the top of a hill, armed with artillery and tanks, gave the population a false feeling of security because the Legionnaires had a well-established reputation of being redoubtable soldiers. The city dwellers believed they would run no risks in hunting in that presumably pacified area.

I was in Da Lat, a mountain city some 300 kilometers (185 miles) from Saigon, so I declined my friends' invitation to join them for the hunt. Da Cruz had also invited two young demobilized military men, who had decided to settle in Indochina as planters. They had been encouraged in that endeavor by the French government, which was still lost in its grandiose dreams of a vast colonial empire. Frenchmen were needed to populate the colonies, so they were given funds to get established in Indochina. We had known these two young men since the time they worked as male nurses in the military hospital in Da Lat, and had taken them often on our hunts.

Once in the rice fields of Cu Chi, the hunters began to position themselves in a straight line, with a space of one hundred meters (330 feet) between them. They turned their backs to the road where they had parked their cars. To their left they could see the Observation Post of the Foreign Legion on a hill about two kilometers (1¼ miles) away, with tanks and cannons guarding the region. Believing that no guerrillas would dare come so close to the Legionnaires, the hunters felt perfectly safe.

The line of hunters slowly advanced toward a bamboo forest half a mile to their front. Da Cruz had already gotten two ducks with one shot. His brother-in-law Paul shot twice at a band of teal flying overhead and succeeded in hitting four birds, which hung in the air for a moment before dropping to the ground. When he bent over to pick one up, a form both human and diabolical rose from the swamp covered with black, gluey mud and bristling with grass and straw from the harvested rice plants. The apparition stabbed Paul in the back with the bayonet on the front of his gun. The wounded man jerked upward, screaming, "The Viet! I am wounded!"

Then he fell back, holding his right side with both hands. His weapon was unloaded, so he could not use it against his assailant. Da Cruz, who was closest to Paul, rushed to his rescue. The Viet ran at him ready to impale him, too, with his bayonet.

"French son-of-a-b—ch!" the man shouted.

Da Cruz caught him full in the face with a load of No. 4 shot. The man dropped his gun, covered his face with both hands, and howled in excruciating pain. A second mud-coated monster appeared suddenly perhaps two steps from Da Cruz, who shot him in the face. At that short distance, half the man's head was blown away.

Paul was throwing up blood. Cécile, a few meters from her husband, made a desperate attempt to reach him, but she could not pull her feet rapidly from the mud, especially since she was weighed down by being six months pregnant. As she slogged her way toward Paul, Da Cruz held her back, afraid other guerrillas might be hiding in the mud. While she wrestled to get away, more Viet Minh rose from the swampy fields. Da Cruz released his grip on her arm to reload his gun. By the time he faced the new assailants, she had reached her husband, who was holding out a hand to her. At the moment her hand gripped his, a guerrilla appeared behind her and thrust his bayonet into her back. Screaming, she fell next to Paul. Da Cruz looked back, saw the Viet stabbing at her, and in a rage unloaded his gun into the murderer's face, which was twisted by hatred. The man fell dead next to his victim.

Believing that Cécile was only wounded, Da Cruz retreated toward the couple and tried to carry her to safety. When he realized she was dead, he left her there and ran toward the road, where his brother José was swapping his shotgun for the U.S. M1 carbine he had left in the car. Thus better armed, he began shooting at the assailants. The two demobilized military men who had been part of the hunting party had run away without firing a single shot. They were supposedly better prepared than the civilians to fight against the guerrillas since they had served in a prestigious regiment famous for the bravery of its soldiers.

We learned later that a food-supply convoy had been scheduled to travel on the colonial road in front of the rice fields. This explained the presence of the Viet Minh in the swamps—they had been hiding in the mud to ambush the convoy. The Sunday hunters had disturbed their plan, and they'd had to retreat into the bamboo forest. Finally they were dispatched by the murderous fire of the tanks sent by the Legion.

When the ambulance brought back the bodies of Paul and his wife, their family saw with horror that Cécile's finger, the one holding her wedding band and her engagement ring, a huge emerald, had been cut off. The thief had not been able to slide the jewels off her finger, probably swollen by her pregnancy, so he had sectioned the finger. The military hospital put the blame on the guerrillas, but we could not see how the "mud men" could have done that. They had been too busy fighting for their lives. It was more likely that the corpse robber was a stretcher-bearer.

After this tragic hunt, the waterfowl hunters ceased their outings in the Cu Chi region. The Viet Minh became better equipped and more experienced, and therefore more dangerous, in the years 1950–1954. They were fighting for an ideal that the colonialists refused to understand. I often heard Frenchmen complain about their hostility.

"What more do they want? We have built roads, railroads, schools, and hospitals in this country. We have provided the natives with jobs and given them the protection and help of France. Is it not enough?" they lamented.

I was surprised to hear such words from the mouths of educated Frenchmen with a high social status. They looked at me with surprise when I would answer, "They don't want France's generosity. They want to be masters of their own country."

After that, surprisingly, my life as a hunter in the high plateau remained the same. I continued to track wild animals in the jungle without being disturbed by the guerrillas, even though they lived there and certainly observed my hunting activities. They probably thought that the death of one French hunter was not worth the risk of compromising the tranquility of the wounded and sick guerrillas sent to recover in Da Lat, where the cool climate sped up their return to health. By killing me, they would likely have incited the French to comb the region in search of the Viet Minh. They had everything to gain by leaving me alone.

Thus I hunted peacefully for many years until I was expelled from the country by the Ngo Dinh Diem family, head of the authoritarian and demonic new regime of South Vietnam. With their unquenchable thirst for power and their corruption, they led this wonderful land, the paradise of my youth, into the arms of the Communists.

# The Mad Elephant of Ratanakiri

## Chapter 8

K'War and I were on the trail of a very big tusker. Those who had seen him joked that his tusks were so long and big that he had to walk backward. That elephant was famous. People called him the "solitaire with a gold-chain necklace." He had belonged to the imperial court of Annam and had an important position as the imperial executioner. His work consisted of crushing the head of the condemned laid on the execution block. One day the huge animal crushed his keeper to death and escaped for the milder climate of the south.

A few hunters who caught a glimpse of him in the jungle said that he had around his neck a heavy chain in red gold, the metal most valued by the Asian people. The necklace, formed by huge links, weighed at least 100 kilos (220 pounds) if not more. The emperor had bestowed the jewel upon the animal to confirm the importance of the animal's position. So went the legend, which became a reality for many people who dreamed of that gold.

Professional hunters as well as amateurs organized safaris to hunt this treasure. They came back telling horror stories about a mad monster that charged without provocation and would crush the head of anyone unlucky enough to be within his reach—as he had done in his days as imperial executioner. Some hunters had fired on the beast from afar, wounding him, but he had always managed to escape. They said he smelled their approach and silently disappeared as if on tiptoes. They added he was like a devil, killing for the mere pleasure of killing. After a while people talked less about the solitary bull, and finally everyone forgot about him.

By then I was already a professional hunter, not only for my pleasure but also for a living. I spent most of my time in the jungle, prospecting new territories. Some of them had never been disturbed by a gunshot. My tracker, K'War, accompanied me in all my expeditions. He was alone now, having lost his wife, K'Put, in a work accident six months earlier. She was coming back from the fields where they cultivated rice and corn, carrying a basket full of rice on her back, when she slipped on the wet mountain trail and impaled herself on the point of a broken bamboo trunk. She could not be freed to be transported to the village, and died after a few hours of excruciating pain. Shaken by the tragedy, K'War could not resign himself to staying in the village with the memory of his wife, and he sought relief by following me on all my hunts. He became my driver, my guide, and my hunting companion.

K'War had all my trust. When he went with me on the trail of an animal, I could see that it took his mind away from his sorrow and he felt less depressed. He was an excellent tracker and rarely lost a trail he was following. I had taught him how to shoot, and learned from him how to read animals' footprints and other signs. Thus, he became a good shot and I a good tracker.

With two other men from Nam Banh, K'War and I set up our camp in a region not too far from Ban Dong along a creek that had almost dried up for lack of rain. A small trickle meandered in the old bed and provided us with pure drinking water. Under the shade of giant bamboo trees we built a temporary roof, a table, and two benches with bamboo trunks. We slept on the white sand of the riverbanks. That place was a green ocean of plants.

But here in the region of Dar Lac and Ratanakiri, we had to be very discreet, since the inhabitants did not like elephant hunters. They made their living from the capture of the huge beasts, and did not give anyone permission to hunt in their region without paying a fee.

I had to pay the village chief a certain amount of piasters in silver coins, which were not easy to obtain. Moreover, I had to provide the village with alcohol and buffaloes. Such expenses made many hunters hesitate to pursue an elephant they had seen a full day before. With the high taxes on hunting added to the bribes to the village chiefs, plus the costs of the expedition, elephant hunters would have to take a big bull with heavy ivory to realize any profit from their hunt. Many hunters, after evaluating their chances, preferred to hunt gaur and banteng, which were easy to find in that region, especially from the backs of domestic elephants.

To avoid the risk of having to pay a large sum of money for nothing—if the beast I was pursuing escaped me by crossing the Cambodian border, for example—I hunted incognito, avoiding villages and other hunters, who, fortunately, were few. I was able to ride easily on old jungle trails in my winch-supplied Jeep. When we found an isolated place, we would set up our camp, from which we would hunt in all directions, including the Ratanakiri, a Cambodian province.

I knew that what I did was illegal, but I had to earn a living. And to survive in my profession I had to kill—very often illegally. I managed to pay my exorbitant taxes, especially when the elephant I tracked died near a village. The inhabitants, always hungry for meat, would always talk about the great hunter who had provided them with that rare food. Their praises sometimes reached the ears of a wildlife department employee. Fortunately for me, each time the administration thought I had been caught killing illegally, I was able to prove that I had paid for my permit, and was going to pay my killing taxes after the hunt.

We were hunting elephants from my camp near the Dray H'ling waterfalls when K'War heard the Montagnards of nearby villages talking about the "mad solitaire." They said this lone bull had a gold chain around its neck and its tusks were so long it had to walk backward. It was said to be crazy because it liked to kill people for pleasure. It had just killed a domestic elephant, working to pull teak logs, and its keeper. The hulking beast was now wandering in the vicinity of Ratanakiri, a Cambodian province.

The Montagnards who had seen the famous elephant talked excitedly about the gold chain and its huge tusks. I hesitated a little. I tried to tell K'War and my bearers that the elephant probably existed only in the imagination of certain Montagnards or, if not, must be dead by now and was the king of elephants in heaven. I could not convince them. K'War was disappointed by my lack of enthusiasm and could not help giving me his opinion.

"It has been one week that we are camping here. We have seen only bantengs and gaurs, and a few elephants not worth shooting. Ông

Tienne, why not go to the Ratanakiri? Even if the mad solitaire with the gold chain does not exist, there are others, and you know that the region has big tuskers."

I had to agree with him, so we left our camp for Ratanakiri, where we would hunt incognito. The dry climate of the region made the hunting grounds easy to travel through because of the lack of leeches. The old jungle trails were very passable with the Jeep, and there were few elephant-back safaris here. I was practically the only hunter in the area, and this was my favorite region to hunt tigers and elephants.

There was no communication between the villagers of Ban Dong and those of Ratanakiri because they did not speak the same dialect. The only times they met were when an elephant carcass was found on the border. Then they would spend the night eating and arguing through two interpreters who communicated in Rhadee, and they always ended up deciding to bury the war axes. I avoided their villages, setting up my camp thirty kilometers (eighteen miles) from them.

We were drinking a pastis diluted with tepid water when I noticed K'War's preoccupied face. He seemed to be bothered by something. I asked each of my men what he would do with his share of the gold chain. K'War immediately replied, as if to unload his mind of a worry.

"Ông Tienne, if *Ông Ba*, the divinities of the jungle, give us that elephant with the gold, I will go and buy K'Put's half-sister. She is living with her adoptive parents in Fyan. I feel too lonely since my wife died. I miss my parents and my friends. And K'Put is haunting me. When I stay a few days in the village, I feel her presence next to me. She calls me. When she was still alive, I thought I was able to hide from her my affair with her sister. But now, she knows. She haunts me and reproaches me every day about my cheating her. What must I do? I feel so lonely and so sad."

I tried to console him: "My good K'War, whether we get that gold chain or not, on our return we will go to Fyan to buy your new wife. If you don't have enough money, I'll buy her for you."

As he started laughing, I teased him: "But what if she prefers me to you when she sees me?"

In a burst of laughter, he spat on the ground as if to say, "She has eyes only for me, old fool! You don't exist for her!"

Everyone laughed and we continued joking. They were good people, and they were my friends. I liked their company. They loved me and respected me. They considered me their brother, as if I were a member of K'War's tribe, the Mâs.

The coffee pot was warming on the embers. I was just finishing my breakfast of a can of corned beef and a cucumber when K'War and the two guides came back from their scouting. They had seen the tracks of the tusker two kilometers (about a mile) from the camp. The animal was walking slowly toward Ratanakiri. I realized that we would have to cross the border illegally, but I also knew that we would run little risk of being caught. We left full of hope.

The region was deserted—no military and no immigration officials. After a few hours of pursuit, we reached an immense savanna full of elephant grass. Getting through it would be a nightmare. We were still a few miles from Ratanakiri province. K'War, carrying my little U.S. carbine with folding stock, led our group. I had used that weapon efficiently on wild pigs, deer, and birds, and also for self-defense. A semiautomatic with ten magazines, each holding fifteen cartridges, it offered substantial firepower, especially when its user was a marksman. A bearer followed K'War with my .404 loaded with solids. I used it as seldom as possible because of the problem of finding ammunition for it. I was next in line, armed with a .375 Holland & Holland built with a square-bridge Magnum Mauser Oberndorf action. That weapon had been ordered by my grandfather many years before, and I was the happy heir of that treasure.

After I checked my .375, loaded with four solids, we walked toward a big noise behind the curtain of tall grass. We knew our elephant was near, although we could not see him. The noise indicated that the five-ton animal was taking a bath in a little pond, splashing water on his body with his trunk and squealing with joy, totally enjoying the coolness of the pond. Heartless, I decided to put an end to his happy hour.

The grass, as sharp as razor blades, was seven feet tall and very thick. K'War and I tried to make the animal stand up so I could see the top of his head and put a bullet in his ear. We started to scream, hoping the giant would get out of the pond. He listened in total silence, then got up and ran away from us. For a fraction of a second I could see his trunk, looking like an enormous leech above the reeds.

We broke through the curtain of grass and fell into the muddy water of the pond, which was about fifty feet across. I had not realized it was so deep. I sank to a depth of about three feet and took a few steps hesitantly. I did not feel stable walking in that mud, and hesitated to go forward. In front of me I saw the passage the elephant had made through the reeds in his escape, his trail splattered with mud that shone in the sun. Seeing my hesitation, K'War urged me to advance.

At that moment the rogue appeared amid a thunder of splintering tree trunks and branches. In all his magnificence and horror, he arrived on me like a tornado, with ear-splitting trumpeting and shrilling squeals. His rolled-up trunk revealed his open mouth, in which I could see a red ball, his tongue. His ears flattened on his neck and his demonic eyes on me, the shiny black mass charged. K'War had disappeared. The mastodon trumpeted again just five meters (sixteen feet) from me.

Instinctively I leveled my weapon and fired in the direction of his huge head. The impact of my bullet stopped him abruptly. He made two or three staggering steps backward and lifted his trunk like a radar device, searching for the source of the painful shock. I reloaded my gun quickly and as silently as I could. The monster advanced toward where I crouched in the mud, and I was about to shoot again when K'War fired three or four shots from behind the reeds into the animal's head. The enraged elephant uttered a shriek that filled me with terror. I had never heard such a noise come from the throat of any animal.

Then the bull saw K'War, who, after firing his four bullets, was trying to escape by wading like a crab through the pond. His movements made a lot of noise, and the elephant focused on my guide and charged—passing so close to me that his foot bumped my leg. The thrashing of the water—and the fear of hitting K'War—prevented me from taking good aim. I saw the rolled trunk lash out like a cobra and hit my companion. I fired. The bullet hit the bull's ear and stopped his charge. He fell on his rear.

I called to K'War and the other men, but the only one I saw was my guide floating facedown in the pond. I tried to turn him on his back, seizing him by the hair to have a better grip. His scalp stayed in my hand. Poor K'War had ceased to live. The elephant's trunk had burst his skull like an overripe orange thrown against a wall. My faithful hunting companion had left this world—no longer sad—and was now with his wife K'Put in a better place where the rice and melons were sweeter than they were in Nam-Banh.

The gold chain turned out to be only a chain made of red copper that had dug itself into the elephant's flesh as his neck had grown larger over the years. It obviously was causing him excruciating pain, and was the reason he was always furious, charging and killing without provocation. He had eight bullets of various calibers in his skull. He had also been shot in the chest, legs, and shoulders. At the base of one of his splendid tusks was an infection swarming with worms and reeking of putrefaction.

All his wounds had been caused by men, and I believe he remembered the humans and their smell when he tried to relieve his pain by immersing his jaw in the water of occasional ponds. And when he had the opportunity, he pursued that smell, the source of his suffering. When he was able to crush a man, his worst enemy, I believe he squealed with delight.

The tusks of that splendid elephant were the most beautiful I obtained in my whole career as a hunter. They are now in my trophy room in North Carolina, always reminding me of K'War, my irreplaceable hunting companion.

# The Man-Eater of Manoï

## Chapter 9

A French proverb says that there are no worse liars than hunters. In a way I agree, but I must admit that there are some hunters who never boast about their exploits. Others do it for them. Most of us feel the need to exaggerate a little when telling a hunting story to make it more interesting. However, the following story is already too horrible and compelling to need any exaggeration. Today, after so many years, I still shudder thinking about those disturbing events.

I had just signed a contract for a safari of thirty days. My client, a rich farmer from Texas, did not know how to spend the huge amount of money the U.S. government had given him NOT to cultivate his cornfields, which extended as far as the eye could see. Someone from the U.S. Department of State, who had been my client, gave a glowing report at his Safari Club on the results of his big-game hunt in Vietnam with me as his professional guide. The rich Texan farmer heard the talk and decided to book a safari with me.

My new client wanted to bag all types of bovines, including gaur, banteng, and Asiatic buffalo. He was not interested in other animals. I decided to take him to Manoï, a Montagnard village thirty kilometers (eighteen miles) from the highway between the station of Krong Pha and Nha Trang. In that area we could find what he wanted: tiger, elephant, deer, and a variety of small and medium game.

My camp had been provisioned with hunting gear and food a few days before he arrived, and my staff was waiting for us. One day before the client's arrival, my chauffeur had brought my Land Rover with the cook, his helper, wine, spirits, and fresh food.

I planned to start our hunting activities by making my client shoot a peacock and a few wild chickens. So we left Da Lat early in the morning in order to be in Manoï at noon. After leaving the highway, I drove slowly on a sandy path and eventually had to cross an almost-dry little river. The wet sand in its bed could have mired down the Jeep for a while, but thanks to the metal sheets I had taken the precaution of hiding in a bush on the riverbank, we made the crossing without any difficulty.

It was ten in the morning and we still had about six miles to go before reaching our camp. Although we were driving slowly under a canopy of giant bamboo leaves, the heat was intense. My client slept in the backseat while K'Sou, my tracker and friend who was seated next to me, scanned the jungle in search of game. As for me, I was dreaming of a cold beer.

My attention was suddenly drawn to a group of Montagnards who appeared at a bend of the trail. I was alarmed to see that all of them were armed with spears. These people never brought their weapons with them when going to town. I planned to stop the car to greet them, but the tense look on their faces made me brake the vehicle violently. They surrounded us and immediately started to speak all at the same time. I signaled that I could not understand what they were saying. They calmed down, and one explained that a man-eating tiger had come the night before and killed a villager, the fourth in a month. He pointed to a young man, the son of the new victim, who sobbed hysterically while trying to give me more details on the tragedy.

I explained to my client what had happened and waited for the young man to collect himself enough to continue. Finally, he said:

"Yesterday we killed two buffaloes and drank many jars of corn alcohol to celebrate the harvest, which has been good. After the feast everyone went to bed, leaving the bloody animal carcasses attached to the sacrificial poles. The odor of burned fat was everywhere. In the middle of the night, my mother, a very old widow, went out into the yard to urinate. We heard the dogs bark, and then came a terrible growl and my mother's shrill scream. I took my spear and my torch and went outside to look for her. She was no longer near our hut. I called her, but she did not answer. I saw a long line of liquid, which appeared black in the dim moonlight, next to a large tiger's footprints. I understood what had happened—the man-eater had come again, and this time had taken my mother!"

I asked whether they had found the corpse and brought it back to the village. He was too shaken to answer. One of his companions talked for him: "We found the corpse at dawn and brought it home. And now we are going to the province chief of Phan Rang to ask him to send soldiers to our village to kill that demon. Since you are already here, we prefer to ask you to take care of this situation."

When he said "demon" instead of man-eater, I thought about another tiger I had shot a few months before in the province of Dông Mé during a night hunt. When my trackers gutted him, they found in his bowels a canvas wallet containing a few bank notes and an identity card belonging to a villager. Full of terror, the guides and coolies declared that the animal was a *malai*, an evil spirit who, according to their superstitious beliefs, could take the appearance of a human being or a tiger. As proof, they had pointed to the wallet. Despite my explanation that the wallet had simply belonged to the unfortunate victim, they stubbornly rejected my explanation.

I was definitely not delighted by the thought of a group of Vietnamese soldiers, armed with .30-06 semiautomatic weapons, patrolling the area to kill a man-eating tiger at the request of the villagers. The soldiers would shoot at everything except the tiger, which they would be unable to find. I would have to move my camp to avoid being disturbed by them. This would cost me additional expenses I had not expected. After weighing our options, I decided to solve the problem myself. I explained to my client what I had in mind, and asked if he would agree to shoot the tiger over a human bait.

He immediately refused: "You know, Etienne, I am not superstitious or afraid of spirits, but the idea of being in a blind fifty feet from a mutilated human corpse in the middle of the jungle, maybe for the whole night, does not delight me. Can't we use an animal bait?"

I explained that a man-eating tiger was different from others. "If he cannot find human flesh, he will eat anything. But if he has the choice, he prefers a fresh or decomposed human, because a human is an easy prey. If I use another bait, he might not come. My choice is to use what remains of the corpse, and as soon as possible."

These poor villagers counted on me and I did not want to disappoint them, but my first duty was to my client. Fortunately, he turned out to be a gentleman, understanding my dilemma and the importance of the situation. He did not object when I told him I would need only one day to solve the problem. I took him to the camp and left him there under K'Sou's care.

Then I went to the village, which was nearby, and asked to meet the chief. He was waiting for me in the victim's hut. When I entered, I was all but choked by a horrible smell. The entrance door, barely the height of a child, was the only opening, and the interior of the hut was dark. There was a lot of smoke, the musty smell of corn alcohol, and that characteristic odor of decomposing human flesh.

After a few minutes my eyes got used to the dark, and I saw a group of villagers around a jar. They were drinking to the departure of the old widow to the other world. Near them was a small pile of embers, from which rose an acrid smoke that made me cough. Behind them I vaguely discerned the shape of a small corpse covered with a bluish cloth on a low bed of woven bamboo branches. Although I felt uncomfortable with all the smells, I asked the chief for permission to lift the shroud to see how advanced the decomposition was. I pulled back what had undoubtedly been the dead woman's most beautiful sarong, which now served as her shroud. A swarm of big green flies buzzed away from the corpse. I stared, petrified, at the horribly mutilated corpse, swollen and full of putrid gas.

The tiger had killed by hitting her on the head. The scalp and one side of the face were gone, leaving thc bones visible through a mass of swollen, greenish flesh. A few locks of white hair still sticking to the skull hid what remained of the face. The corpse looked alive under the ever-moving mass of flies. One leg had been torn off at the loin. I was so nauseated that I could no longer examine the cadaver. I turned to the chief who, along with the victim's son, had the authority to allow me to use the corpse as a bait. He invited me to his hut, where I found the woman's son and relatives and friends. They were all noisy and seemed drunk as they received me joyfully, which in my opinion seemed improper under the circumstances.

According to the rituals, they offered me a dose of alcohol in a jar. The chief handed me a tube through which I had to suck the alcohol mixture—polluted with insects and worms that still clung to the leaves they used as filters. It had the taste of sour cider. I could not offend them by refusing, but I would not list it among my favorite drinks. I finished my dose stoically, then passed the tube to the man next to me. Then I asked to speak.

I explained all the good reasons for using the corpse as a bait to draw in and kill the man-eater. Everyone was horrified. Those primitive people believed more in the power of the dead than in the power of the living. Such a profane action would bring evil on the village, they said. At that precise moment, the regular rhythm of the mortuary gong could be heard—reminding the villagers of how often they had heard it during the last month. I took advantage of that macabre music to ask the chief and the family to make a rapid decision. Acting with all the prudence and diplomacy I could muster, I told them I had to return to my client the next day. I played my last card by saying to the chief, "If this tiger is not killed soon, he will take other victims, probably one of you and maybe tonight. I will wait for your answer at my camp."

As I got up to leave, the son and the relatives decided to agree. I could not help silently admiring the wisdom and the courage of these people. They had strong beliefs, but also much common sense. Since they were responsible for the fate of the whole village, they made the difficult choice to take on the risks of profaning the dead. The village chief and his assistant promised me all the assistance I would need. I requested six men to construct a blind and transport the corpse. They accepted, and the work started.

The victim had been found in a bamboo grove some three hundred yards from the village. The tiger had left her there because the villagers had approached close to his refuge. I chose precisely that place for the blind and the bait. To avoid alerting the tiger by making changes in his familiar environment, I sent the men well away from the site to cut the branches and leaves for the camouflage.

Once the blind was finished, at 3 P.M., I went back to the village, preceded by my six coolies. I wanted to return to the blind and hide inside the camouflage before five o'clock, the favorite time for the tiger to start eating. I went to the victim's place and suddenly found myself alone. The men who had worked for me had disappeared as if by magic. No one came when I called out. I rushed into the hut. Except for the cadaver and a dog sniffing at it, nobody was there. I thought that perhaps the son and his relatives were getting drunk again in some neighbor's hut, so I went back to the village's gathering place, which seemed deserted. Even the dogs and chickens that usually crowded this place had disappeared. The whole village seemed to be shrouded in a malevolent atmosphere, heavy and hot. I had the impression that the air itself was vibrating—perhaps it was the torrid sun or the regular beating of the gong.

I was filled with a sudden rage against the superstition of those people. At the top of my voice I called for K'Sou. He arrived a few minutes later with my client. I felt relieved to see the American, who personified civilization and a rational world. I sent K'Sou to the village chief to tell him that I would abandon the whole project if I did not get more help in the next ten minutes. K'Sou came back accompanied by the chief and a young man, the village idiot. With their help I rolled the corpse in a blanket and we tied it to a pole carried by K'Sou and the idiot. My client did not want to watch our work, so he returned to the camp to forget that nightmare with a glass of bourbon. I followed the funerary cortege to the blind.

On the way I came across two of the men who had built it and asked them to come help us tie the bait to a tree. They looked at me as if I were crazy and then fled as rapidly as their legs could carry them. I insulted them in their dialect and threatened to abandon their village to the tiger. The fear of a malevolent spirit, however, was stronger than the fear of impending death. They did not answer and disappeared. I was alone with K'Sou and the idiot, who laughed silently while watching the interplay. We untied the ropes and I rolled the corpse out of the blanket by pulling one end. The corpse stopped with the face turned upward. K'Sou and his assistant jumped backward. The idiot screamed in terror. Believing that he, too, would soon disappear, I nearly panicked myself.

In the face of the dead woman, only one eye was visible, the one on the side where the bone was bare. That eye seemed huge and alive, and gave the face the look of a Cyclops. The other eye was swallowed up in the swelling of the wound and the decomposition. One arm, certainly broken, was completely twisted. From the missing leg a few pieces of bones protruded like daggers. In the emaciated chest, three deep cuts were open to the ribs. For a moment the jungle itself seemed petrified by the horror of that sight. The deathly silence that had suddenly fallen on it was broken by the noise of a vulture taking flight and by the hissing of gas coming out of the corpse.

I cut a long rattan vine and made a slipknot, passing it around the neck of the corpse. With another vine I fixed the twisted arm. The work caused me to touch the cadaver several times. Contrary to common belief, the cadaver was not cold but hot. Its shiny skin seemed about to erupt. I worked like a robot and did not pay attention to anything else, so impatient I was to finish my task. I pulled the vine around the chest too tightly and heard bones break and a long hissing—it was almost as if the old woman was trying to scare me. Panic and disgust overwhelmed me when I received in my face the putrid smell of the gas and saw at the same time the only eye fix on me. Shaking, I tied the corpse to the tree and covered it with the sarong.

Finally I returned to the camp with my helpers. My client was taking a nap. I was soaked in the smell of decomposition and was sure the horrible odor emanated from me. Without eating, I drank three glasses of rum, offering some to K'Sou and the village chief, who had come to the camp after the return of the idiot to the village. Somewhat fortified, I took my .375 Holland & Holland loaded with four softnose bullets, a Thermos of hot coffee generously mixed with rum, and my gear bag with my electric headlight and extra ammunition. I refused the hot pies made by the cook and went off to the blind with the village chief and my guide.

It was 5 P.M. I was sure that the tiger would not come to the bait until dark. I entered the camouflage and warned K'Sou, "No one should come to the blind for any reason. After you hear my signal, you come with four bearers to get me."

He closed the door of the blind and they made a lot of noise while returning to the village. But instead of the usual loud conversation, they started the funereal song dedicated to the dead of the mountain. I lay motionless and alone, like a dead man in his coffin of leaves, and listened to that gloomy litany become fainter and fainter in the distance. After a while I got up on my knees and watched through the aiming window. After all the emotions of the last two days, I seemed no longer to be a civilized man, and was suddenly invaded by an unreasonable fear. The old woman's head was turned toward the blind, and the bloody wound on her face extending from her ear to her mouth made her look as though she was smiling at me and staring at me with her one open eye. Her hair started to float around her skull, and the foul odor became more intense.

The sarong partly covering her flew away. I imagined that she was getting up to come toward me. Only my pride and whatever shred of reasoning power I had left held back the scream of horror in my throat.

I drank several cups of the scalding coffee, which brought me back to the earth and reality. I lay back on my blanket and realized that I had waited in a blind many times, over various baits, though none had the awful smell of the decomposed human flesh. I almost felt poisoned by these odors and gases. I felt feverish and started to fall asleep but, from long habit, forced my mind to remain alert. I listened intently and realized that the humming noise made by the flies swarming over their macabre banquet had stopped. The silence was sometimes broken by the sad and gloomy call of a peacock, answered by a gibbon with a derisive laugh. All the animals were getting ready for their nocturnal rest or activities.

Night set in very suddenly. I removed the leafy window, in the middle of which my trackers had cut a hole. I wanted a better view of the target. A civet cat was on the bait, crunching a bone. Time passed. I must have fallen asleep when I felt a presence. The tiger had come. Something in his silent approach had alerted my senses. I tried to make him out.

I heard his powerful jaws tearing the bait, and leaves rustled as he shook the tree, trying to break the bait free and take it to a place where he could enjoy it more comfortably. He did not like the place where I had tied it. Silently I mounted the six-volt light on my head. I took my gun, aimed in the general direction of the bait, and turned on the light.

The bright beam illuminated the hellish scene: The tiger, his eyes phosphorescent, stood on the chest of his victim, his jaws clamped on the head he had just torn from the body of the corpse. The woman's long white hair hung on each side of his muzzle like a sinister mustache. With half of his corpse in the dark, he looked like a monster from hell. I aimed and fired just below the eyes, which turned away. With a menacing growl, he charged toward the beam of light—the apparent cause of his sudden pain. My blind collapsed and I found myself in the open, barely covered by a few leaves. I reloaded and fired almost at random through the branches. Luckily I hit him in the chest and he fled.

For a few minutes I heard him growl and rattle. Then he was silent. Thanks to my lamp, I found him lying dead some distance from his headless victim. When K'Sou and the bearers arrived, we looked for the skull. It lay a few feet from the blind, like a football abandoned on a field. The tiger had summoned the strength to go more than one hundred meters (over three hundred feet) with two bullets in his corpse, one in the neck and the other in the chest.

He was a magnificent animal but a poor trophy. The man-eater had only three legs, which explained why he attacked a human instead of the wild animals that could run away faster. Everything ended at dawn. The tiger's body, minus the skin, was burned to ashes to appease the malevolent spirits and the human victim.

I sent the tiger skin to my taxidermist in Da Lat. After resting a night, I took the tracks of a herd of gaurs with my client. I went thirty-six hours without eating, haunted by the smell of the corpse that remained in my nose. I found in my camp a spear and a jar, gifts from the good Montagnards, who would always thank me in their own way. Later the men of Manoï village would tell their children and grandchildren of the exploits of Ông Tienne, the killer of the man-eating tiger.

# My Campaign for Velvet Horns in R'Pouma Klong

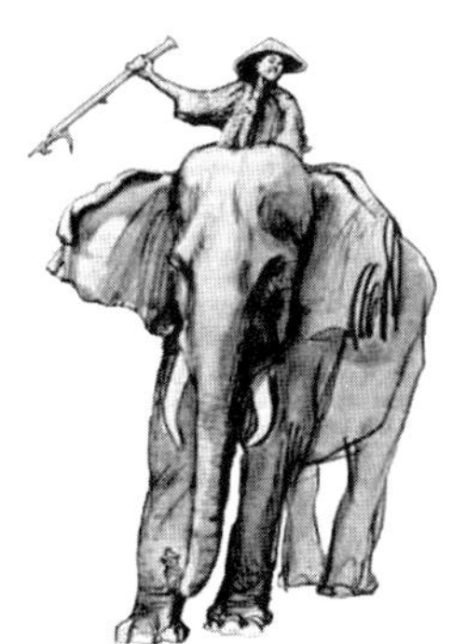

## Chapter 10

Every year during March, I would wage my "campaign for velvet horns" of the swamp deer. These antlers were and still are highly prized by Chinese druggists for their aphrodisiac properties. The male swamp deer weighs at most 70 kilos (150 pounds). His fur is similar to that of the sambar, and his meat is coveted by gourmets. He usually lives on the borders of swamps, and goes to rice fields at dusk to eat the water plants. He sheds his antlers from February to May.

That's when I would make my two-month-long expedition into the plain of R'Pouma Klong. During that time I shot not only deer, whose horns I sold to Chinese druggists, but also tiger and elephant. The deer meat I prepared as pemmican—first I would season it with lemongrass, hot pepper, salt, black pepper, sugar, fish sauce, and rice alcohol, then expose it to the sun until it became dry like leather. Because the superstitious Montagnards did not eat deer, I employed a team of two Tonkinese (North Vietnamese) families—parents and their children—to help me gather the meat, and I sold them fresh venison for half the normal price, which they would then dry to make pemmican. (One hundred pounds of meat, once dry, does not weigh more than 10 pounds and thus was easy to transport.) My Tonkinese specialists needed 200 kilos (440 pounds) of big game every day to make pemmican. So I killed swamp deer, sambar, buffalo, and banteng. When they had enough pemmican—and enough bearers to transport their meat—they went back to the cities to sell it before returning for a new supply.

At that time of year the dry season started. All the animals moved closer to the water holes and would graze in nearby pastures. I shot the deer and the buffaloes in early morning or late afternoon because night hunting became dangerous in the dry season. All the water holes and swamps were gathering places not only for animals needing a drink but also for poisonous snakes, most of them cobras, that came to feed on frogs living in humid cavities. These were king cobras, with an average length of two meters (six and a half feet). I killed them for the region's Montagnards, who loved the meat and would barbecue it on their open fires. Often, using my M1 carbine, I got cobras longer than eleven feet. A famous American hunter, Col. Charles Askins, wrote in his book *Asian Jungle, African Bush* that he had seen specimens over 18 feet long. I believe him.

As mentioned, I avoided hunting at night. The guides refused to follow me into those snake areas, and most other hunters also chose to avoid them because they were far from civilization—the village of R'Pouma Klong was a two-day walk from the highway. It was difficult to find bearers and guides for a safari into this lost world, but a few professional hunters like me preferred it. I felt free as the wind there—I came and went as I wished.

Besides the snakes, the only problem was the place had a bad reputation—it was believed to be haunted by evil spirits. Many of the inhabitants, both men and women, were sick with goiter and pellagra, almost certainly caused by a deficiency of iodine in the thyroid gland. That's why it was so difficult to find bearers. Hunters who had some knowledge of medicine gave me this advice: "A goiter is not pleasant to look at, but it's not contagious. Pellagra is another matter. Avoid close contact with sick people if you don't want to look like an old python in its skin-sloughing period someday."

In that hunting area one could find all kinds of game—elephants, the three bovines but especially the wild buffaloes, tigers and panthers, and birds, including all kinds of pigeons, wild chickens, and peacocks. I shot the birds only to supply the camp with meat. I had the opportunity to follow the tracks of a rhino, but I did not ever see it. The tracks led toward a Viet Cong stronghold, and a band of them stopped me and asked me questions. However, that political movement did not wage war against hunters. They only wanted to topple the rotten Diem government. They invited me to share with them some dry meat—which they had probably bought from the Tonkinese families. They knew I was hunting in the region and that I was harmless. I declined, however, believing it was safer to stay away from them. I left the rhino tracks and went back to my camp, dreaming about the fortune I could have made from the rhino's horn, which was worth one million piasters (about thirteen thousand dollars) in 1959.

I built a new camp for each expedition. Both the hut and the furniture were made from bamboo. I always chose an attractive place under the canopy of giant bamboo near a river. Even in the dry season the rivers always had a trickle of fresh water. I would dig a hole in the sand of a riverbed and it would fill with water, giving me both a bathtub and a refrigerator for my cans of food and bottles of wine. I stored carrots, celery, and turnips in the humid sand of the banks. I went to the village for tomatoes, eggplant, hot peppers, and the lemongrass I used for my infusions in order to save on tea and coffee.

In front of the camp's sleeping room was a covered terrace open on three sides, which served as my living and dining room. The kitchen, built in the same style, had a partition allowing the men to sleep in one room while the cook prepared meals in another. The latrine, a deep hole into which my guides poured lime every three or four days, was well away from the camp. Because of the difficulty of finding bearers, I reduced all my equipment, food supply, and weapons to a minimum. I needed many bearers to carry coarse salt, alum, kerosene, and rice alcohol (used as a gift to obtain services from the village).

My armament included an 8x60 Mauser carbine with double trigger, 6X riflescope, and 100 solid and softnose bullets; a .404 Jeffery Mauser with 50 rounds of solids; and a Model 70 Winchester .22 Hornet with 300 cartridges. As a defense weapon, I also had a .30-caliber U.S. carbine with folding stock and ten magazines of fifteen cartridges each. I always carried both offensive and defensive hand grenades, which served mainly for fishing in the river.

The camp of the Tonkinese families was far away. Their meat, as it dried in the sun, attracted swarms of flies, although it was strongly spiced with lemongrass and hot pepper. During my expedition I would shoot an average of thirty swamp deer (only males), ten sambar deer, and two or three bantengs. All those animals went to the Tonkinese. As bait for tigers, I would shoot two buffaloes, and sometimes I would use an elephant if it did not die too far away from my camp. One of my trusted trackers and some men from the village would search for the herds of big game. They would leave early in the morning and come back in the evening to make their report to me, which was almost always positive. Sometimes, when a storm was brewing, we could hear elephant trumpeting. This made hunting them easier, for we knew from the start in what direction to go.

During each of my two-month expeditions, I would shoot two or sometimes three tigers, an average of two elephants, about thirty deer, and two bantengs. On one expedition I shot three elephants, the second triplet of my career. In Indochina one found elephants either in a herd or as a lone bull, never in small groups of several bulls, as occurs in Africa. Therefore, I was lucky to find the three males together and just 10 meters (30 feet) from each other. All three were good tuskers, yielding a total of 75 kilos (165 pounds) of ivory. I earned a lot of money from my expeditions but, alas, did not hold onto that wealth for long. Two months of privation in food, alcohol, and sex led the hunter to excesses. As a result, I was never rich.

The plain of R'Pouma Klong was famous for its tigers and buffaloes, which represented the great majority of the big game. In 1957, during an expedition of forty days, I brought back five tigers, of which two were males 3½ meters (11½ feet) long from the muzzle to the tip of the tail.

When I remember that expedition, I cannot help thinking about my old friend Georges Rochelle. He had a tea plantation that did not bring him enough money. To earn more, he took Americans employed by the diplomatic mission in Saigon on safaris.

One day, by a stroke of extremely good luck, one of his clients shot one tigress and its four cubs. The word *tigron*, meaning a tiger cub, did not exist in the vocabulary, but a few hunters sometimes used it. Georges was proud of his prowess and did not stop bragging about that massacre. Each time I met him in a bar, he retold the same story, how his client had shot five tigers in twenty-five minutes. One evening, our friend Plas, who had drunk too many glasses of pastis, said to him before a group of friends, "You know, Georges, you are confusing me. I cannot remember whether your client killed five tigers in twenty-five minutes or twenty-five tigers in five minutes."

Poor Georges! He died in his bed of a bilious fever instead of being devoured by a man-eater or crushed under the feet of a big gaur. He is now hunting in a paradise where tigers are even bigger than they were in R'Pouma Klong and come to the bait by the dozens.

# An Encounter with the Viet Minh

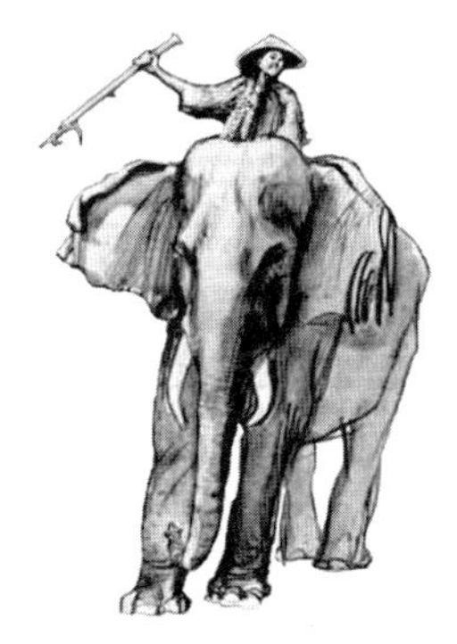

## Chapter 11

Early in my hunting life I did not have enough money to buy a Jeep, the ideal vehicle for hunting and transporting game. Therefore, I worked out an arrangement with the ticket collector on the Da Lat–Nha Trang train, who in turn obtained the complicity of the engineer. The base of my operations was the station of Krong Pha. The Chinese owner of the station restaurant where I regularly took my meals let me rest in a little room there before I started on my safaris. After shooting my game during the night, I had it transported on oxcarts to Dông Mé or Krong Pha before noon the next day. There we put the game in a vacant freight car and I took the train to Da Lat. A rented truck waited at the station there to transport the game to the schools and orphanages with which I had contracted to deliver meat. I had to pay only 10 percent of the sale price to transport one ton of meat.

Everything was well organized and synchronized. When I had to hunt in areas far away from the station, my accomplices would let me board the train at any station where I waited. My hunting territory was the immense plain of Krong Pha, where the Song Pha River meandered. My favorite places extended from Krong Pha to Tan My and Dông Mé, and from Krong Pha to Manoï, villages that were very accessible to the oxcarts that I used.

I would leave the station at 3 P.M. with four men and two carts, heading toward my hunting areas. Sometimes I saw bantengs late in the afternoon and would shoot them, ending the hunt right then. At other times I hunted by night, shooting game with the help of a headlight. I never came home from my hunts without game. Nobody but my helpers knew about my hunting areas. We went through a sandy plain with some forest, or through extended forests of *bang-lang* or *dâu* trees. Sometimes I would spot a herd of elephants. If I had the time I immediately shot one of the animals. If the herd was far away, I would take a chance and wait until dawn to pursue it. Then I would send a cart to let the ticket collector know that there was nothing to put into the wagon that day. In the morning, full of courage, I would run after those elephants in the hope of finding a few big tuskers.

On the banks of the Song Pha River there were beautiful forest clearings where I almost always found banteng or deer at dusk. In the dry season I would camp on the sandy riverbed and during the monsoon on the rocks of the riverbank. Often, after leaving the station, I was able to get the quantity of game I needed even before reaching my hunting area.

We would set up our camp on the bank of the river, start a fire, and cook our dinner. During my night hunts I noticed something very interesting: The noise made by the oxcarts seemed to intrigue the wild animals. Instead of fleeing, they would stay put, apparently fascinated by our convoy. As for me, if I already had the necessary quantity of game, I would just watch and go on my way.

One day I was lying on a mat in my cart as we moved slowly toward the banks of the Song Pha. It was still early, and I decided we should set up camp in the forest near some huge rocks. At that place the opposite bank was three hundred yards from our bivouac. The terrain was flat and thinly covered with small *bang-lang* bushes and dwarf bamboo. I was cleaning the lenses of my riflescope when I saw a convoy of several oxcarts beyond the river on the side of Bidup Mountain. The carts seemed to be heavily loaded—the animals were walking slowly. Some ten men in charge of the convoy spent their time yelling at the animals and whipping them to make them advance. The men were dressed in black, like the Viet Minh guerrillas.

To see them better, I leveled my carbine to look through the scope and was surprised to see a man seated on the opposite bank looking at me through his scope. He certainly thought I was military because I was dressed in the camouflage uniform of the commando parachutists. In two seconds he got up and gave a command, and I heard a deafening explosion behind me. They had fired a mortar shell, which fortunately had fallen behind one of the big rocks and had not destroyed anything.

When I realized they were Viet Minh and were firing on me, I loaded my 8x60 with military Mauser ammunition. Those cartridges did not cost me anything and functioned perfectly well in the 8x60. I filled the magazine with two incendiary and two perforating bullets and aimed at the first cart, which I could see carried several cans of gasoline or kerosene. My first bullet, a perforating one, hit a can. My second was an incendiary bullet that transformed the cart into a torch. The oxen, crazy with fright, ran toward the river. A few bursts from a Browning automatic rifle were followed by silence.

I got out of my hiding place and watched the opposite bank. There was my observer behind his binocular. I waved at him with my hat. He must have realized that because three hundred yards and a river separated us, I with my carbine and scope and incendiary bullets was the winner in this firing game. He answered with a sign of his hand, and the convoy disappeared in the distance.

To gain more security, I changed my plan. I returned to the train station, hunting on my way back. It was a few months before the end of the battle of Dien Bien Phu between the French and the Viet Minh, and I learned later that the same convoy traveled every fortnight to get supplies at the village of Krong Pha, where there was a post of railroad guards.

The guards were former military of all army branches who lived with, and often had illegitimate children by, native female villagers. The guards could return to France with their tickets paid by the government, but their illegitimate families could not accompany them. To help their French men, who had only a miserable salary, the women sold their merchandise to anyone who would buy it. (They did not care about politics.) The chief of the post, a former adjutant of the Legion, was aware of the clandestine commerce but preferred to ignore it because this was the eve of the truce.

I don't know how that Legionnaire heard about my shooting contest with that band of Viet Minh, but he did. Because that band was welcomed at Krong Pha, he forbade me to come to the station. I had to change hunting areas, so I went to the village of Tan My, where I stayed in the hut of one of my trackers. I hunted and organized safaris in that region until 1960. At that time the area became a military zone occupied by the South Vietnamese army, which eventually killed off much of the country's wildlife. Soldiers who had never had weapons until then used their M1 Garands, Enfield .303s, and Mass 36 guns to hunt whenever they had the opportunity.

In 1958, if one walked half a mile away from the highway into the forest, it would sometimes be possible to see herds of wild bovines during the day. Deer, muntjac, and wild boar were common sights. Rabbits, pigeons, wild chickens, and peacocks existed in great numbers. Until 1960 one could buy, at the markets in Da Lat, Nha Trang, or Saigon, hundreds of doves, rabbits, and francolin partridge that had been caught in traps set by the Vietnamese villagers or the Montagnards. One year after the occupation of that zone by the army, you could not see even one single monkey—only vultures circling and a few doves flying very high. That one-time hunting paradise was essentially empty of animals.

Another paradise soon to vanish was the famous plain of R'Pouma Klong. After the war, the new regime in Vietnam decided to transform that zone into a reservation for all game. I wish them good luck. Opening land to tourists means easy access with good roads for cars.

Many inhabitants still secretly own weapons such as the M16 or AK-47, and they will not resist the temptation to hunt with them. After years of uncontrolled poaching, soon only cobras will be left in the region. I might be wrong in saying so, however, because the Vietnamese appreciate frogs as a delicacy, and they hunt these small amphibians. But frogs are a staple of the snakes, and without the frogs the cobras will also disappear. I sincerely hope that the AK-47 and the M16 of the communist regime will not cause havoc in R'Pouma Klong the way the M1 did in Krong Pha.

I hope also that the present regime in Vietnam will be willing and able to protect the wildlife and the forests of that wonderful country. On 25 August 2004 a Vietnamese friend gave me some good news: A law now stipulates that anyone killing a gaur will go to jail. No longer will someone be able to use the excuse of self-defense because a gaur was angry or threatening. Big-game hunting is no longer permitted. A few privileged people have permission to go for snipe and doves, which exist in abundance to the south of Ho Chi Minh City, in Da Lat, and on the Lang Bian Plateau.

# The Haunted Hunting Fields

## Chapter 12

Sometimes after a hunt, I would sit with my guides in the middle of the jungle or in one of their huts. As night fell, we would sit in front of a flickering campfire sipping Caravel rum and smoking cigarettes. They smoked my black Bastos tobacco and I smoked American Dominos. When I ran out of Dominos, my Montagnard friends would give me tobacco that they grew themselves. We smoked it before it dried completely, and the cigarettes smelled so bad that they drove the mosquitoes away. We talked about our former hunts and all the incidents, funny or tragic, that made them memorable.

One evening a very old Montagnard, who my guides said must have been at least one hundred years old, joined us while we were relaxing in their hut. As we talked about various hunting areas, he suddenly interrupted us with a quavering voice, saying only one word, "*Maya*." The father of my two young guides and several other older Montagnards became attentive, waiting for the old one to express himself further. The others did not seem to consider his words to be the ramblings of old age, so I also gave him my attention. He took his time, chewing some black tobacco with his toothless gums, and said that in his youth he had seen "*mayas*" in certain parts of the forest.

"What were those *mayas*, grandfather?" a young guide asked politely.

"Animals with long, pointed teeth in a human face," the old one replied. "They were like giant bats, and their bodies ended with a tail they twisted around a branch. Hanging upside down, they snatched all creatures, animals or humans, who passed below them unaware and devoured them. The victims came back to a ghostly life in their former shape to wander aimlessly near the place they had been killed. A hunter could shoot at those *maya* animals, but he would never get his game because they would disappear without a trace. One could see them running, but they left no footprints on the ground."

Although I could not believe what he said, the old hunter's young audience was listening closely. My guides did not make sarcastic comments or smile with skepticism. I had known all the villagers since I was ten. They were my friends, so I respected their beliefs, even though my Western mind was unwilling to admit the existence of ghosts. It was the first time I had heard about the *mayas*. I didn't assume, however, that the old man was talking nonsense. I thought instead that I might learn from his experience so that I would be able to deal with a *maya* if I happened to see one. The fact that I had never been confronted by *mayas* didn't mean they did not exist. Nothing guaranteed that I would not see them one day. And this old man had managed to stay alive after such encounters.

"What do we do if we see a *maya* hanging upside down from a tree?" a young guide asked.

"Don't go near him," came the answer.

A few years later I had the opportunity to hunt with Jean Da Cruz, my friend from childhood, in a plantation that had been abandoned by the owner, whom we knew well. He had left the region after a fire burned his house to the foundation. The jungle had reclaimed the beautiful plantation of 300 hectares (600 acres). Nothing remained of the house but a magnificent floor covered with Italian marble slabs, around which thorny bushes grew. The inhabitants of Fyan village, five kilometers (three miles) from the house, wanted to come and take this marble to cover the dirt floor of their huts. They often talked about the project to encourage each other. But nobody dared come near the plantation, which they believed was haunted by French and Viet Minh soldiers killed in the battles that had taken place here.

Jean Da Cruz's tracker, like all the other Montagnards, had heard about the *maya* ghosts that haunted the plantation, so he was not very happy about accompanying us on this hunt. What made him change his mind was the sizable salary he would receive from my friend for his services. When we reached the plantation, the tracker could not help looking everywhere with fear. We noticed his strange behavior and began to taunt him.

"K'You, look over there. A French soldier is peeing against the tree. Do you want us to go and see whether he is a ghost?"

K'You became pale while glancing toward the place we pointed out. He knew we were making fun of him but was not too offended, since we had always treated him as a friend. Finally he started to study the terrain for gaur tracks. The villagers of Fyan had told us there were many herds of gaurs in the area. For two hours we walked on ground covered with new grass—usually a telltale sign that the vegetation had been recently burned by a forest fire. The ground, wet from a morning rain, revealed fresh tracks left by a herd. I showed the footprints to K'You, saying, "Those prints are clear—no *maya* herd left them."

He did not answer, but spat on the soil, then pinched his lips into a smile that meant, "Don't talk too soon about what you don't know!"

We hurried in the direction the footprints led us. Twenty minutes later we saw about twenty gaurs grazing peacefully in a green pasture about a hundred yards away. From our position we had a good shot at these huge targets. I had a .404 rifle and Jean a 10.75 Mauser. To get closer for a sure shot, we hid behind bushes of bamboo burned by the recent fire and approached within about a hundred feet of them. The herd contained three or four young males worth a shot, plus about ten females and small calves.

I chose a male that had a horn spread of some 85 centimeters (33 inches). Jean chose his and waited for me to shoot first. I pressed very steadily on the trigger and fired. To our surprise, not one animal moved. I fired again. The young bull I had chosen lifted its head, looked at me for one second, then ran ahead of the herd toward the border of the bamboo forest. Jean and I both reloaded quickly and fired together at a bull that was still grazing and presented his side to us. The two bullets made a big hole in a small tree beyond the animal, and we assumed that our bullets had gone through the body of the bull, which disappeared with the other gaurs into the forest.

We ran after the animals, whose tracks were very visible. We had to stop, however, just before reaching the bamboo because there were no footprints anywhere in the last thirty feet of open ground between us and the forest border. The whole herd had disappeared into thin air, and yet we were sure they had run into the bamboo.

For two hours we walked with our noses to the ground, looking for tracks in the damp soil, but found none. We knew it was dangerous to go after gaurs—especially wounded ones—in the middle of dense forest vegetation because they could charge from a short distance without our being able to fire accurately at them. We were so frustrated, however, that we decided to follow the herd anyway. We moved slowly, fingers on triggers, trying to detect any sign that would reveal the presence of the animals. K'You, the expert tracker, searched intently for signs of the passage of a herd of huge animals, such as broken branches and crushed bushes, but he could see nothing. Under the bamboo, the silence was thick and oppressive. All of us also felt something evil around us. Jean and I looked at each other and agreed to end the pursuit.

Once in the open air, my friend said with a sickly smile, "I guess we were after *maya* gaurs. Not surprising they disappeared from under our noses."

I kept repeating, "I am *sure* I hit that bull!" I was shaken by the bizarre incident. I could not bring myself to accept the mysterious disappearance of the gaurs, or that I had missed that large target at a distance of only a hundred feet.

Later, a similar misadventure happened to me in a nearby region. I had set up my hunting camp about one hundred kilometers (sixty miles) from the haunted plantation in a place that abounded in gaurs, tigers, and elephants. I was preparing to receive a safari client from the United States. The day before, I had killed a female gaur to use as a bait for tigers, and had given some of the meat to the villagers of Pool, not far from there.

I was walking with my brother-in-law, André, an inexperienced hunter who had never heard about haunted hunting fields. He was excited by the idea that he was going to shoot a sambar deer or a gaur as bait for a second tiger hunt. He was armed with my new carbine, a Brno 8x60 Mauser. Two weeks earlier, I had received some Belgian-made hard point and softnose ammunition. It was new and reliable, not like the ammo made in France by Grasset, which misfired three times out of ten. I certainly would not recommend it for hunting elephant or gaur. Any guide following a large animal wounded by a client would be in mortal danger if his cartridges misfired.

André left with my guide, K'Sou, armed with my .30-caliber U.S. M1A1, with ten magazines of fifteen cartridges, which I often used as a weapon for self-defense. My own rifle was loaded with softnose bullets. I knew the area like my own pocket. I was very thirsty and had not brought anything to drink, so I decided to head for a good creek that I knew.

As I approached that place I picked up the characteristic scent of gaur (I was gifted with a keen sense of smell and could catch big-game odors from a great distance). Alerted, I moved ahead noiselessly and soon saw the black, shiny body of a gaur. He was a lone bull, and though his horns were not impressive, he offered a ton of good venison close to my Jeep, so I would be able to transport and sell it to the butchers in the city, or even sell it at a low price to the villagers of Fyan, thus helping me to pay the crew I needed for the safari.

The animal was just 50 meters (165 feet) from me. Between us was a creek, so the running water would cover any noise I made during my approach. The gaur, busy eating water plants on the bank, did not sense my presence. I rested my rifle on a branch of a dwarf oak. Though I was a sharpshooter, I took all precautions not to miss my target. The gaur presented his side—I could not miss him. I carefully aimed and fired. The animal did not even move. I saw the impact of my bullet beyond the bull—bark on the trunk of a large pine tree flew into the air.

The old bull continued eating, showing no sign he had heard the rifle's detonation. I reloaded quickly, making a slight noise. Still he ignored me. I fired again, with the same result. This time, however, he lifted his head and I saw his malformed horns. He stared at me for a long minute, then turned away and disappeared into the bamboo bushes. I did not hear any noise of his retreat into the forest. Elephant hunters, when they lost the game they were tracking, would say jokingly, "He must be walking on his toes." But neither an elephant nor a gaur can disappear in complete silence.

André and K'Sou, hunting not far from where I was, eventually joined me. I saw that K'Sou was preoccupied with something. I told them what had happened to me and said to the guide, who knew me well, "I am sure, K'Sou, that we are going to find him."

"Are you positive, Ông Tienne, that it was a gaur? Did you see bloody tracks?" Then he added, "I won't go after him, because he's a *maya*." And he spat vigorously to make his words more definitive.

I insisted that he help me, but he refused to move. I knew he was brave, since we very often hunted together. He had never hesitated to follow with me the tracks of a wounded animal, but now his wisdom told him not to confront the mysteries of the other world.

My brother-in law told me he had fired the five cartridges in his magazine at a huge sambar deer, but not one had exploded. The absence of tracks seemed to confirm the presence of *mayas*. It was André's introduction to the haunted hunting fields. He asked me why, since I was aware of these ghosts, I hunted in the region.

"I wanted to check for myself the truth of those rumors," I replied. "This is my second experience with ghostly animals. I'm starting to believe they exist, but I haven't seen the *maya* itself, a creature with the body of a bat and a human face. I need more proof to believe it really exists."

Regretfully I left that region, even though I loved it, and knew I would never go back. André suggested jokingly that I bring my client there if he wanted a second gaur. "He will waste his cartridges, and you will not run any risks going after a *maya* gaur," he said, laughing.

"The problem," I replied, "would be to convince a tracker to go after a gaur. I don't want to follow one of those animals myself—not because I am afraid of ghosts but because you never know what could happen if you confront a dark power."

I did not make fun of the haunted hunting fields because I had proof of their existence. However, I avoided talking about them. I knew the mentality of hunters, who loved to criticize each other for missing their targets. I could imagine them saying, "Oggeri is very smart. Now each time he misses a tiger or a gaur or an elephant, he will say they are *mayas*."

The French have a proverb: "Words are silver, but silence is gold." Therefore, I did not tell anyone about my misadventures with the ghostly animals, but neither did I laugh with skepticism when my friends the Montagnards shared with me their experiences with the other world. I sometimes thought I would like to meet the *maya* with a human face and a bat's body. I would not miss him with my .404, and he would make a very rare trophy.

A few years later, I read a military communiqué in the press about the baffling disappearance of a company of Legionnaires in the mountains of North Vietnam. The soldiers, who were well armed and equipped with radios, had disappeared into thin air. No signs of a battle, no bodies, no empty shells were found. The Legionnaires had not radioed their command post to request more troops and artillery support. The post in the area had not heard a single detonation of mortars or machine guns that would have indicated a fight with the Viet Minh. The mysterious disappearance of an entire company has never been explained.

I also read a story about the Zulus of Africa. It described how Prince Matana, son of the great king of the Matabeles, in the company of the famous general Pugana, had led an army of ten thousand soldiers into the forest of Mafungabusi along the Zambezi River in pursuit of the Barotses, enemies who periodically raided their lands. That huge army had disappeared without a trace. Scientists, history professors, and other educated and knowledgeable people had studied the extraordinary case without finding an acceptable explanation to that mystery. Nobody could accuse them of being stupid, superstitious savages.

Thinking today about those baffling mysteries, I believe it might not have been a good thing for me to have encountered a *maya* during my hunts. I, too, might have disappeared into thin air. On the other hand, I might instead have become a ghost like the gaur I had missed, and perhaps turned into a *maya* hunter, wandering in my beloved jungles among the giant bamboo for eternity.

# My First Triplet of Elephants

## Chapter 13

During another memorable hunt, in the immense plain of Riong Tho, I succeeded in killing three sambar deer. Two were females, each weighing more than 120 kilos (265 pounds) after being emptied of the entrails, and one was a big male. The male was a *daguet*, so called because its horns had no offshoots and looked like two daggers. That huge sambar weighed as much as the two females put together.

After wading all night in the rice fields and vast swamps full of aquatic plants, which particularly attracted deer, I went back to the village where I had set up my hunting camp. My friend Jean Da Cruz had preferred to stay there and wait for me rather than hunt by night. He said he was afraid of breaking his leg walking in the dark, but I think he was afraid of missing his targets. Not many hunters could place a bullet between the eyes of a deer at a distance of sixty or one hundred yards at night.

In the pale light of the following dawn my men found fresh tracks of a small herd of elephants going in the direction of Fyssun village, where there was another large pond covered with aquatic plants. I immediately ate my breakfast and prepared a substantial snack, for I had decided to go after the elephants, even without being sure whether the herd contained a male with big tusks.

Jean, who had never shot an elephant, wanted to be part of this hunt. I entrusted some men with the job of transporting the deer I had killed to Riong Serignac village, where I had left my Jeep. They would have to quarter the animals, line the floor of the car with layers of banana leaves, put the meat there, and cover it with a coarse canvas to protect it from the sun because I did not think I would be back from the elephant hunt before 3 P.M. Jean could not help me shoot elephants with his 1892 Berthier, but he could supervise the removal of the tusks. I paid these men, and we hurried off.

The mud left on the leaves by the passage of the elephants was still wet. By 7 A.M. we had reached the edge of an immense forest of maritime pines circling the big pond. We stopped there to look around. The sun, having risen to the top of the trees in front of us, was like a giant ball of orange candy that dazzled us with its bright beams. I told my trackers to walk to the left of the pond where the ground was dry instead of wading through the water as they were planning to do. The pond was shallow, but the sticky mud on the bottom would slow them down. Just as I finished my instructions, we heard elephants trumpet. A few seconds later three of them appeared on the far side of the pond, hulking monsters with their gray, metallic skin shining in the sun. All three were bulls. They were alone and had not seen us. They walked calmly in our direction, stuffing aquatic plants into their mouths as they came. I did not go to the trouble of sorting out which was the biggest—all had tusks impressive enough to be called decent trophies. The animal in the lead knelt down in the pond. The two others, a little farther off, continued to eat without showing any sign of alarm at our presence.

I had replaced my .404 Jeffery with a .375 H&H Francotte, for which it was easy to find ammunition on the market. This rifle was a marvel of the Belgian arms factories, made by a master gunsmith. It had an octagonal 26-inch barrel with a Westley-Richards front sight, an express rear sight with five folding leaves and a large V opening, a Mauser Oberndorf Magnum action with one trigger, a stock in finely veined Circassian walnut, and dull bluing. The gun was so accurate that I was able to shoot without support and hit an orange at 100 yards. I never used a scope with big-caliber guns.

My rifle was loaded with four solid Kynoch bullets. I flipped off the safety and walked bent over toward a bush of lotus plants. I broke off two or three large leaves and, using them as natural camouflage, progressed toward my prey. When I was about thirty yards away, the animal, alerted, got to its feet. The other two joined him and they all walked rapidly in my direction. I looked behind me and saw Jean, who had not taken the precaution of camouflaging himself and was thus in full view. I aimed and shot at the nearest animal, hitting him between the eyes at the swelling of the trunk. Slowly he dropped to his knees, apparently dead. His companions ran away in panic, but soon came back and smelled the dead animal. They lifted their trunks and moved them from side to side, trying to find out where the danger was coming from, then ran away trumpeting. I fired again, hitting a bull in the ear hole. He fell dead on the side on which the projectile had hit him.

Behind me Jean was struggling like crazy with his 1892 Berthier carbine, which kept misfiring. He reloaded but again had a misfire. He swore at the French weapons and their unreliable ammunition, and I saw that he would not be able to help me shoot at the third elephant, which was already over one hundred yards away and showing me only his rear. I fired at the base of his tail and probably broke some vertebrae. His behind collapsed like a heap of gelatin; with his front legs he made desperate attempts to get up while stridently trumpeting his pain and rage. I ran to him to deliver the coup de grace. When I saw his magnificent tusks, which crossed each other, the words of the Marquis de Monestrol, a great hunter, popped into my mind:

"Etienne, if ever you encounter an elephant endowed with a pair of unusual tusks, especially if they are crossed, shoot him, but very cleanly. No repeated and poorly placed bullets, no butchery. Never forget he is a prince of the jungle."

A few meters from me, Jean continued to swear and vent his rage on France: "Not surprising that France lost the war against Germany and now is losing against the Viet Minh. Their weapons have been made to *lose* a war, not to win it!"

That princely elephant gave me 27 kilos (nearly 60 pounds) of ivory. The tusks of his companions weighed only 15 kilos (33 pounds) and 11 kilos (24 pounds) per pair, respectively.

While admiring those trophies, I suddenly realized that I had a big problem: Jean and I did not yet have our A permits for big-game hunting. The three elephants killed in the middle of the open plain were going to attract the attention of the nearby villagers and the gamekeepers. I would have to hurry to town to obtain our permits and, if possible, make a deal with the official in charge of selling licenses. He was a friend—I had supplied him with cartridges for his old Darne gun.

I explained to Jean what I was planning to do. He agreed to put two elephants on his permits since I would be paying for everything, the permits and the taxes. While driving my Jeep back to Da Lat, I thought about the best way to solve my problem. Failing to do so would be catastrophic: My hunting license would be suspended for three years, and I would be fined for killing big game without a permit.

My gloomy thoughts improved as I passed in front of Gargantua's Inn, the restaurant at the airport. I remembered the wonderful fresh chitterling sausages it had served me earlier with mashed potatoes and yams accompanied by an excellent 1947 Graves white wine. At that time I could resist everything except temptation. Therefore, I stopped.

When I entered the small restaurant, the owner, an old Vietnamese who knew me well, came to me wiping his hands on his whitish apron and asked with a broad smile, "Well, Monsieur Etienne, still the same thing?" He still remembered what dish I had come to savor in his restaurant (which was renowned even in the capital). We shook hands and I sat down at a table.

"Yes, Ông Than, always the same thing, but this time instead of two sausages I would like to have four with very strong Colman mustard."

While waiting for my order I imagined the four plump white chitterling sausages sizzling in goose fat in the frying pan, and I could already smell their aroma before they appeared on the table. What a delight! I drank two glasses of iced Graves wine in rapid succession with the wonderful dish.

The chef there was an ace of French gastronomy. Where had he learned to prepare his pig meat? To season his sauces? The old Vietnamese chef had fought in World War I alongside French soldiers. After the war he had learned to cook French food before returning home to his country. Today, after forty-six years of searching in the United States, I have not yet found any fresh chitterling sausages as good as those I ate in Da Lat that day.

As I paid for the two hunting permits, the office clerk asked me, "Monsieur Etienne, you are leaving for your ivory campaign? How many elephants are you going to kill this time?"

I felt guilty about the three elephants I had killed without a permit, and I had the impression he was alluding to my unlawful action. I replied, "Yes, Mister Phuoc, I am leaving for one month, but I would like to pay my license fees in advance and those of my friend Da Cruz, so I won't have problems with the military patrols in my area. Could you please let me pay now for, let's say, two or three pairs of tusks?"

With a smile, he said, "And if you don't kill any elephants? What would I do with the money? I cannot give you a refund."

"It's very simple. I wouldn't dare to bother you for a refund if I come home without a trophy. You have already helped so much by permitting me to pay in advance. Do what you want with this money. If someone asks you how many elephants I paid for, please say three, but otherwise don't volunteer any information. By the way, I have here two boxes of 00 buckshot cartridges for your Darne gun. I almost forgot to give them to you. I know that you have been short of ammunition for a long time. Use them sparingly. The new regime doesn't allow weapons or ammunition to be imported. Only my American hunting clients can supply me with them. So be careful! Don't go hunting a *con nai* (deer) for Tet (Vietnamese New Year). You know that night hunting is forbidden."

He realized that I knew about his own illegal activities, which could cause him problems with the government. So he agreed to the somewhat illegal transaction I proposed. That is how I obtained my permits and my right to kill big game. Now no one could find fault with my hunting activities—I was innocent as a newborn.

It was 4 P.M. when I passed again in front of Gargantua's Inn on my way back to camp. Believing that my friend Da Cruz would be hungry, I stopped there to order a big Bayonne ham sandwich for him and buy a few bottles of fresh beer. Jean was not a gourmet and appreciated quantity more than quality. He would certainly like this sandwich.

As I waited for the chef to prepare the snack, the director of the airport, an old colonist, came to my table. After greeting me, he asked, apparently a little annoyed, "Monsieur Oggeri, is that you who shot the three elephants in Fyssun? Hundreds of Montagnards are coming from nearby villages with their backpacks to quarter the three animals and get meat for their pemmican. The DC-3 pilot of Emperor Bao Dai saw the huge crowd from his plane and sent a radio message this morning. He asked us to inform the authorities so they can start an investigation and find out who is responsible for this massacre. That person himself will inform His Majesty."

"Yes, my friend and I are the guilty ones. Da Cruz shot two elephants and I shot one this morning at seven o'clock. I returned to Da Lat immediately after the hunt to pay the license fees because I am planning to stay several days in the area and use the carcasses as bait to get one or two tigers. This year I won't have to leave my safari to go back to town, as I did last year because the leader of the military patrol did not know the hunting regulations, which allow a hunter to pay his license fees only at the end of his expedition. I have learned my lesson, and so I paid before returning to the jungle."

"If you have the opportunity," I added casually, "could you please tell the pilot of the flying taxi to be wise with his old *coucou* (bird) and leave the hunters alone. Some of them might be trigger-happy because of the presence of the Viet Minh in the forest."

Then I got up, took my beer and sandwich, and smiling sarcastically I thanked him for thinking of me as being "guilty" of the massacre of those elephants. The three bulls became a popular subject of conversation among Vietnam's hunting amateurs. They all agreed that it was very rare in Asia to encounter a group composed of males only, and that such small herds existed only in Africa.

Three months later, my brother-in-law, André, wanted to accompany me and try out my new CJ-5 Willys Jeep, which was less comfortable than my Land Rover but faster. While I drove the road from Krong Pha to Nha Trang, he sat comfortably on the passenger seat and studied the roadside for banteng, gaur, and sambar. In the years 1949–1959, we could sometimes see these large animals in that area between four and five in the afternoon. Suddenly my attention was drawn by shadows moving in the darkness of the jungle. I could not make out whether they were animals or men, so I sent out my tracker, K'Sou. He came back soon after to report that the moving shadows were elephants.

I took my .375 H&H Francotte loaded with Kynoch solids and led K'Sou, armed with a .30-06 Garand, on the tracks of the herd. My brother-in-law left his comfortable car seat for a harder one—a tree branch six yards off the ground. He explained his decision with an embarrassed smile and the words, "It's better to foresee than to cure."

I was again on the ivory trail, and this time, four bullets resulted in four dead bull elephants! I do not call this shooting feat a "quadruplet" because the animals were not killed together. I had to follow them and take them one after another. Their tusks certainly could not be called trophies, but they brought me some money. At that time I killed for a living, not to collect trophies.

# The Blue Tiger of Kala

## Chapter 14

The mayor of Da Lat invited me to his office "for an urgent discussion," his messenger said. When I arrived, the mayor was in conversation with the province chief of Djiring. Both seemed preoccupied, but they welcomed me with a large smile and outstretched hands. I was surprised by their friendly attitude since I was well aware that I was on their blacklist. One pushed an armchair toward me while the other poured me a glass of whiskey. *Aha*, I thought, *they really need my help for something.* They started the conversation by thanking me for coming so rapidly. *Hmmm*, my mind was buzzing, *the problem must be a serious one, and I must be the only one who can solve it.*

I knew they hated me. Their hostility had begun a few months earlier. I had given a ride to two young French women who were having trouble climbing the ascending road leading to the center of Da Lat town. I was in my old Jeep, which had several times been repaired by Vietnamese mechanics who had some magic ability to make trucks of the 1920s function. The women told me they lived in Saigon and would be in Da Lat for the weekend. They accepted my invitation to spend the evening with me. We first went to the best restaurant in town, La Dauphinoise, whose owner was my friend F. Modini. He served us tripes à la mode de Caen with a good bottle of Graves and, of course, did not make me pay cash. He knew that my night was just starting.

Everything happened as I had planned. The women ended the evening in my apartment, drinking another bottle of Sahel red wine. When I took them home, it was five in the morning. I was surprised to discover that they were staying in an apartment above the mayor's office. It was there that the government official would bring white females who accepted his paid invitation to spend a few days in his company and that of his male friends. The men had apparently spent money on those two women, and I, the playboy of Da Lat, had spoiled their planned sex party. I understood that I was now their *bête noire.*

For this meeting, however, the mayor and the province chief had put on a smiling face to camouflage their hostility. They explained to me that a man-eating tiger was causing havoc in the region of Kala, a small leper center for the Montagnards not far from Djiring. The mayor said that people were afraid and nobody dared to go there to shoot it. I interrupted him to let him know I was not duped by his words.

"Kala is the leper hospital for the Montagnards of the high plateau of Lang Bian. All the lepers have to go there whether they like it or not. The hospital is kept by the Sisters of Charity under the guidance of Monsignor Cassaigne, who just died from the disease that he loudly proclaimed was not very contagious. People are not afraid of the tiger but of contracting Hansen's disease (leprosy), and you want me to go among the lepers to shoot a tiger that is perhaps contaminated? I heard that the tiger dug up the dead to eat them and that he sometimes eats the patients who go outside to relieve themselves. No, sir. I don't like the idea of going there. I will let someone else have the honor of killing that tiger."

But they insisted, telling me they would pay any price I wanted for the job. I jumped on that opportunity and replied that I did not want money but an authorization signed by the province chief to hunt in the backcountry of Kala toward Phan Thiet along the Gia Bac trail. I obtained the right to hunt for one week in that region, along with permission to kill two elephants for which I would not have to pay license fees. I was in heaven because I knew there were very big tuskers in that area. Perhaps for that reason, the province chief had prohibited any hunting in the area.

The mayor and his friend asked me not to reveal our deal and offered me another glass of whiskey. I left the town hall in good spirits. I knew my new friends would not say a word, even if I killed five or six elephants.

I made preparations for the unpleasant task and left with my faithful companion K'Sou for the kingdom of the leper-eating tiger. My first visit there would be to the director of the hospital, operated by the Sisters of Charity. When I told her I was planning to use the corpse of a patient as a bait, she almost fainted. I explained there was no other solution if she wanted to spare the living patients under her care a violent death. She promised to let me know as soon as a patient died. I set my camp about a mile from the hospital in a place that did not smell too much of the disease. Maybe it was my imagination, but a strange odor of decomposition and medicine seemed to float in the air. It was a sinister smell.

My three bearers and K'Sou did not feel comfortable living so close to the lepers. I must confess that I myself was not as relaxed as I usually was being as close as we were to patients painted in blue (the lepers had to be rubbed daily with methylene, a blue medicine that helped to dry out the ulcers from the disease).

Early in the morning I went to the hospital for news, but no death was expected for the moment. I took advantage of the respite to send K'Sou and one of the bearers to get information about the movements of elephant herds in the region. I gave him my little carbine to shoot a peacock or some wild chickens. K'Sou frowned and spat on the ground to show his disgust, and he asked with some irritation, "Are you going to eat the birds around here? Everything here is carrion, even the living animals. Did you notice the odor of those two nuns when they came to speak with you? The odor of carrion was all around them—they smell like tiger bait!"

When K'Sou came back in the evening, he announced that several herds were in the region. They had been there for several days and their sign was visible in the rice fields behind Bryan Mountain. Another larger herd—at least sixty animals including some big tuskers—was about twenty kilometers (twelve miles) away. I was impatient to finish my job with that man-eater and get back to my favorite big game.

I was about to eat my breakfast when the head sister [head nurse] arrived accompanied by a young nun. They told me of the death of a leper, who would be buried that same day after the ten o'clock mass. I offered them some coffee, which they refused. They could smell the cognac I had mixed in the coffee, and they could barely conceal their shock over the smell of that good spirit in the black liquid. They apologized and invited me to lunch. I accepted.

After they left, I went with K'Sou to the cemetery, where the gravediggers had already started their work. I told them not to dig deeply—my tiger might abandon his prey if it was buried too deeply. Then I went to the refectory where several sisters, Vietnamese and French, were having lunch. I was surprised to recognize among them a young blonde girl in her early twenties, which was about my age. We had both been teenage members of my uncle's nuptial cortege in Nha Trang. I was about fifteen then. We had liked each other and had started an innocent flirtation. She recognized me and blushed when I squeezed her hand affectionately.

The lunch was abundant, but I had difficulty eating the chicken and vegetables tended by lepers. The young Montagnard woman who waited on us already bore the characteristic symptoms of the disease, including swelling of her face and ear lobes, red spots on her forehead and cheekbones, and the curled-up little finger of her right hand.

The good sisters noticed my anxiety and tried to reassure me that the disease was not so contagious as many believed. They could not convince me. I told them about their beloved and venerated Monsignor Cassaigne, who had died from his exposure to leprosy.

On my way back I told the gravediggers again that it was not necessary for them to cover the body with clothing or too much dirt. I had my blind built at the edge of a thick bamboo grove a few meters from the grave. The dead body was lowered into the hole and covered with only a few shovelfuls of dirt. I watched all the poor sick Montagnards who attended the funeral ceremony. It was a nightmarish scene. They were all blue from their daily application of methylene medicine, and looked like the Tuareg nomads of the Sahara, who would turn blue from the indigo used to color their clothing. I was struck, however, by the hope that still shone in their eyes in spite of their terrible disease that led to a slow and horrible death.

After the funeral cortege had left, I entered the blind with my rifle, my headlight, and a Thermos full of coffee mixed with cognac. I lay down on a mat. K'Sou closed the door of the blind and took off toward the hospital with a few lepers who were beating rhythmically on a gong. The sound of that music was sad and sinister, but the tiger knew it was a signal that a good meal was waiting. He was not far from the graveyard—I had come across his huge footprints and blue droppings near a pile of human bones, including skulls, tibias, and femurs. I had informed sister superior of this pile so that she could have the bones re-buried.

Around 2 P.M. the cat made his appearance. He was very large, and not handicapped by any wound or old age. He went straight to the new grave and started to dig with his front paws. In five minutes he had unearthed his prey. I put a solid into his cervical vertebrae, and he fell dead on the spot. As usual, my bearers and my guide rushed to me after the shot. They started to tie the animal to a stout pole, but stepped back with horror when they touched the huge paws.

Like his whiskers, the triangle of his muzzle, and the inside of his mouth, including the gums and tongue, the soles of the tiger's paws were blue. The blue flesh he had eaten for so long had transformed the animal into a true "blueblood." I succeeded in convincing my men that he was not a *malai** tiger, and that the medicine taken daily by the sick had tinted his own flesh. I had his skinned body buried but brought back his fur and sold it to a tourist, who found the explanation of the blue paws intriguing.

After renewing my supplies in Djiring, I left along the trail from Bryan Mountain to Phan Thiet. In two days' hunting I shot three good-size tuskers. The sale of their ivory and the tiger's skin made me forget that for a few days I had flirted with the bacilli of a slow and horrible death.

*A *malai* is an evil spirit that can take the appearance of any human or animal, which allows the evil spirit to get close to its victim and kill it. A *maya* is an evil spirit with a human face and bat's body, and the victims of these evil spirits come back as ghosts.

# The Hunt That Tolled the Bell for Me

## Chapter 15

For a second time I checked the work being done on my Jeep by my driver and a mechanic. I had to leave in the morning for the jungle to build a hunting camp for a new safari, install three blinds, and shoot some deer to serve as tiger baits. The French ambassador had chosen my safari company for his tiger hunt, after hearing it praised by many of my former clients.

The contract I had accepted was rather difficult to fulfill because of the diplomat's busy schedule. Because he had social obligations he could not miss, he would be free to wait in the blind only on certain days. We had agreed that he would stay in the city while I remained in the jungle. I would hurry to town to get him as soon as a tiger began to eat a bait. We would still have plenty of time that day to wait in the blind for the animal and shoot it.

Everything was ready for my trip to the jungle at 6 A.M. the next day, so I went home to take a bath. I was surprised to see my friend Khiem waiting for me. He was the brother of Madame Nhu, President Ngo Dinh Diem's sister-in-law, who gave herself the title of first lady since the president was not married and she performed the duties of his hostess. Khiem said he had come on urgent business.

"Here you are," he said, "the Great White Hunter, the man everyone talks about in Saigon for his hunting performance! I've met the director of Shell Oil Company, who wants you as his guide. He is planning an eight-day safari for after Christmas. But we'll talk about that later. Clean yourself up quickly—right now I am taking you to meet another client, a woman. Groom yourself carefully because she likes handsome men. Hurry up."

I told him I would need at least one hour for my bath and to get myself ready.

"Too long," he protested. "Wash your hands, and we go. Keep your hunting uniform on. It suits you very well even though it's a little dirty with spots of car grease."

"What's this woman's name?" I asked, full of curiosity. "Is she young? Old? Does she know how to shoot? Has she ever hunted?"

"You'll see for yourself. Hurry up because I have an appointment with the mayor after this visit."

I was ready in ten minutes. I had washed my hands and doused myself with Roget & Gallet cologne, but had not been able to remove the smells of gasoline and grease that clung to my clothes. I said to Khiem, "If the client likes strong smells, she will be well served with my cocktail of cologne and gasoline and grease."

Twenty minutes later we arrived at a magnificent villa built in the French Riviera style in the middle of an exotic garden. Orchids hung from trees awaiting the time to bring forth their blooms, which would come in five weeks on Tet, the Vietnamese New Year. An artificial brook meandered along a well-manicured lawn, with rocks as big as a car to indicate the brook's source. Among the flowers I could see a few small, tame deer and civets. Small monkeys and squirrels lived in the trees. In the center of this paradise was a beautiful Japanese kiosk made of scented wood and bamboo where one could sit to drink aperitifs. I thought, *This woman, whether young or old, must be very rich and an interesting prospective client for future safaris.*

Khiem said nothing, but his lips revealed a light smile as we walked toward the house. He had been my childhood friend, so I knew that the smile was an indication that he was planning to play a trick on someone. I had the feeling that I was that someone. My curiosity was aroused. *What did he have in mind?*

When the door opened, I could think no more, so dazzled was I by the woman. She took my breath away. In my mind I compared her to a sparkling diamond. In a glance I saw everything of her: her small "Tanagra"* body, slender and flexible, dressed in a white fencing uniform, her curled black

*Tanagra is a small Greek village famous for the excavated figurines of beautiful women.

hair falling to her waist, her pale pink lips half open over very white teeth as she greeted Khiem. As she put her arms around his neck, I noticed her beautiful hands, well-shaped fingers ending in long fingernails covered with a silvery varnish. For a reason I did not try to analyze, I felt relieved when she gave him a brotherly kiss on his cheeks.

"Good morning, beautiful little sister," he said. Looking toward me, he added with an amused smile, "Lechi, I bring you someone who is not a stranger to you. Do you recognize him?"

She looked at me with perplexity, shaking her head, and said, "I believe I saw him one day on the road to the Couvent des Oiseaux, but. . . . "

I also remembered the pretty woman driving a black Peugeot I had seen that day while on my way to sell venison to the convent. I had promised myself to do everything I could to see her again because she had aroused in me a feeling I had never experienced before, but I had not been able to find her. And here she was. I came out of my daydream when I heard Khiem say to his sister, "It's Etienne Oggeri. Don't you recognize him?"

"Etienne! I remember him as a little boy with round cheeks!"

"That was more than fifteen years ago. Now he has grown up!" Turning to me, he said, "Etienne, this is my sister Lechi."

As she stretched out her hand to shake mine, I saw in my mind's eye a scene from my childhood. We were a group of children playing in my mother's garden. Khiem's parents had rented the big house my mother had put on the market for that summer. During the rental time our family lived in her boarding house across the garden. Khiem had two sisters, both of whom looked very serious, like all Vietnamese young girls of that time. I heard that one of them was even engaged to a young lawyer with a bright future from a very wealthy family. I was twelve years old and small for my age. My younger sisters were already a head taller than I. Khiem was perhaps a little older, and always had elegant clothes that I envied. When we rode horseback together, I wore old shorts and rode bareback like an American Indian, but he always used a saddle and wore well-tailored riding pants and leather boots.

His sisters never played with us, but one day one of them wanted to climb a prune tree to pick the fruits instead of making them fall to the ground with a long stick. She carried a small basket and had a problem getting up the tree. I happened to be nearby, so she called to me, "Etienne, can you help me?"

I helped her the best I could by putting my hands under her armpits and trying to lift her, but she was too heavy for me. She tried to put her legs and arms around the tree trunk to hold on while crying to me, "Push, Etienne, I'm going to fall!"

I wondered how I could lift her. There was only one way: I would have to put my hands on the fleshiest part of her body. I did so and then, with a tremendous effort, was able to lift her. To gain an additional point of support, I put my cheek on her right hip. She urged, "Push just a little bit more—I can almost grab the branch over my head."

I felt her little behind shake in my hands in her efforts to reach the branch. Suddenly her pants, made of fragile silk, got caught on a twig and were torn, revealing the flesh of her hip right where I had put my face. I slightly turned my head, and my lips came into contact with her cool, firm, and perfumed skin. The pleasant sensation whipped up my energy. With a powerful push I lifted her, and she clung to the branch. Holding it firmly, she climbed the trunk until her feet were level with the branch; then she threw one leg over and straddled it. We looked at each other, out of breath, and she burst out laughing.

I wafted back into the present and heard the same laugh coming out of the lips of the pretty woman who watched me with twinkling eyes. As if she had seen the images that had come to my mind, she put her hand in mine and asked, "Do you remember the day when you helped me climb the prune tree?"

"I'll remember it all my life."

I was telling the truth—I had never forgotten that scented flesh on which I had put my lips for a short moment.

"You would not have any difficulty lifting me now. You are so tall, strong, and virile, and you are tanned like an American Indian," she said, looking at me appreciatively. That string of enthusiastic adjectives revealed her candid and innocent joy in finding a friend from childhood. Her words went straight to my heart, and her delightful spontaneity swept me off my feet. I saw myself as she saw me—tall, strong, virile, and redoubtable, and fully equipped physically and emotionally to protect the exquisite woman she was. I fell instantly in love.

My eyes locked with hers. I felt my blood pulsing rapidly at the thought of my hands on the fleshy part of her body—such was the image she evoked.

Lechi was in the middle of a fencing lesson with her two daughters. She apologized to the fencing-master, a young lieutenant of the South Vietnamese army, for the interruption and asked him to continue the lesson with the little girls. We sat down in a corner of the room and talked about her future safari. She said she had never hunted, never shot a rifle, but even so she wanted to be the first Vietnamese woman to collect a tiger and a panther, the two trophies coveted by all big-game hunters. I promised to see her as soon as I returned from the jungle in three days and give her her first shooting lesson. I also promised to make her a crack shot.

When I shook hands with her upon leaving, I felt a kind of electric current run through us. She had aroused in me an intense desire to possess her. She had bewitched me, and I decided to use whatever bewitching power I myself possessed to make her mine. She would be my possession and my drug for life.

As he took me home, Khiem asked, "What do you think about your new client? If you want to please her, bring her orchids and wild animals. I am convinced you have made a good impression on her. I know my sister well."

"I'll bring her the first prunes from my garden."

"*Prunes*?" he exclaimed without understanding.

I just smiled without answering him.

I spent two days in the jungle to finish preparing the safari for the ambassador. I had tried to shoot two or three sambar deer for the three tiger blinds. Unfortunately, the north wind was so strong that it carried my scent to my prey, so I was not able to approach the animals close enough so as not to miss them. Moreover, my headlamp's beam did not reach far enough. Since I could not obtain wild animals, I had to buy two domestic buffaloes from the Montagnards. I had not included that extra expense in my contract, but I thought the ambassador was rich enough to reimburse me without objection. It would cost him only three thousand extra piasters to get a tiger skin, which was worth twenty thousand and sometimes more.

When everything was ready for the hunt, I went back to the city, where Lechi was waiting for me. Before seeing her, I had to talk with the ambassador, who spent the weekends in a beautiful villa provided for diplomats by the French government. The man received me with open arms, so happy to see me that I almost expected him to have a red carpet thrown before my Jeep. He was with two corpulent and haughty men. They must have wondered about this unshaven man in a hunting uniform who dared interrupt the ambassador of France in the middle of a conference.

The ambassador introduced us. I learned that they were the military attaché and the French consul. They shook hands condescendingly with me. I was invited to have a glass of wine, and my client asked point-blank, “Can I go to the blind tomorrow? You see, I’ll have the whole day free until eight in the evening, when I must have dinner with several foreign diplomats. After that, I’ll be able to go back to the jungle and stay there until five o’clock in the afternoon of the next day, which is Christmas Eve. I’ll be busy the whole day on Christmas with invitations and golf. We could go back to the camp afterward and stay there for one or two days. This is my schedule. What do you think?”

“I must first tell you, Mr. Ambassador, that I had to buy two buffaloes to use for baits. I was not able to shoot any deer because of the strong wind, which carried my scent to them from afar. I could have tried to shoot at them, but I did not want to risk wounding them because they would have gone to die in the bottom of a ravine where the tiger could find them. Then he would no longer need to feed on the bait near the blinds. With the buffaloes, your safari will cost you three thousand piasters more than we expected.”

“What? Three thousand piasters more? But you are supposed to provide the baits! I don’t see why I should pay for them now.”

I tried to calm his rising anger by smiling and fully explaining the situation: “Yes, I was supposed to provide the baits. But we are in a different situation. I had no control over the bad weather that prevented me from shooting bait animals. Knowing how busy your schedule is, I did not want to postpone your safari. These two buffaloes were absolutely necessary for you to get the tiger, so I bought them. I am willing to share that unexpected expense. I have spent more to prepare your safari than I have ever spent for any other client because I had to hire two groups of trackers to visit the blinds every day in order to know as soon as a tiger comes to the bait. I must manage things very carefully to make sure you get the animal in the few hours you can come to the blinds.”

“I don’t want to pay this extra cost,” he said, “even if it’s only one-half. Here is a check for the initial amount we agreed upon.”

Without taking it, I calmly said, "Sir, not one other guide would have organized a safari for you with the restrictions you set. In normal conditions a hunter must remain with me in the jungle from the beginning of the hunt until the moment he shoots the trophy. I guaranteed your hunt and still do, even though I have never seen a hunter come to the blind one day, be absent two days, and come back the fourth day. I will accept your check, however, if you add half the amount I had to pay for the buffaloes. I still guarantee you the tiger if you come with me now to the camp and stay there until I show you the animal."

I could not help adding with a smile, "To be really sure you would not miss him, you should perhaps send him your card with your schedule."

"Mr. Oggeri, I don't appreciate your kind of humor. The more I think of it, the more I am convinced that I don't have to pay for the bait."

"In that case," I said icily, "you won't pay for anything—no bait, no safari, no tiger. I'm breaking the contract. Don't worry about the camp I have already built for you. I have another client who will pay for the bait and shoot your tiger, or I'll kill it myself. Next time you want a safari with me, you'll have to give me all your time."

I stood up and walked out under the angry eyes of the three high-ranking officials. From that time on, I had only contempt for that French ambassador. I did not know at that time how much he deserved my contempt.

After my visit to the diplomat, I went directly to Lechi's house. She was ready for the shooting lessons I had promised her. I took her to the jungle on the edge of the city. In two days she assimilated my directions so well that she was able to hit a pack of cigarettes from a distance of one hundred yards with my little .30-caliber U.S. carbine. I told her about breaking my contract with the ambassador, which opened up the chance for her to get her tiger in three or four days, if she could leave for the camp with me right away. She accepted enthusiastically and without any hesitation.

I came back two hours later to get her, but before leaving for the jungle, I invited her to have lunch at La Dauphinoise's, and we dined on tripes à la mode de Caen and spaghetti à la Bolognese, served with a bottle of Chianti. Our conversation was easy—we talked like two friends without flirting. I could not help thinking, however, that I was going to have with me in the narrow confines of the blind the woman I desired, and I tried to control the ardor in my eyes so as not to risk scaring her. Deep down, my instinct told me that she was attracted to me, too, although she did not show it.

Three hours later, we were on our way to the camp when we saw my tracker K'Sou on his bicycle. He was coming to Da Lat to let me know that the tiger had come to the bait. We took him back to the camp with us in the Jeep. It was 3 P.M. when I reached the blind. The footprints left by the animal were barely visible, so I deduced that they had been made by a young tiger or a panther. I asked Lechi whether she wanted to shoot an animal that did not seem very big.

"A young tiger or a panther is still a beautiful trophy," she replied enthusiastically.

"Well, then, we'll have to spend the night in the blind to wait for it to come back."

We took our places in the small camouflaged shelter made with bamboo and roofed with branches, spreading blankets and a mattress on the floor, which I covered with DDT powder to keep the insects away. I reminded Lechi about what she would have to do in order to shoot the animal either during the day or at night. Then we lay down silently side by side on the blanket.

It was cold, so I handed her my flask of St. James rum. She took a sip of the strong drink without making a face. She seemed to enjoy everything. Though I had been close to very many women before, I was in an indescribable state of excitement and confusion. It seemed my blood was boiling and my ears ringing. My jaws hurt as if I had a toothache. This exciting creature lying close to me consumed me so totally that at first I did not hear bones breaking between powerful teeth.

The wild beast we were expecting was there. Silently I signaled its presence to Lechi, then took the .375 H&H loaded with softnose cartridges and handed it to her. I peered through the small aperture to see what animal she was going to shoot. It was not the tiger she wanted but a pretty spotted panther. I whispered in her ear, "It's a panther—do you want to shoot it?"

Her lips formed a silent "Yes."

"Stay calm. Push the barrel of the gun through that small opening without touching the leaves, aim at the shoulder, and shoot."

She put her cheek on the side of the gunstock, aimed, and pressed the trigger. The recoil made her fall on her back; she dropped the weapon, rubbing her chin and cheek. I had not foreseen that the recoil of the powerful gun would be too strong for her little body. The detonation was deafening and the explosion made the withered leaves of the blind fall on our heads. I quickly looked through the opening: The panther lay dead next to the bait.

I congratulated Lechi and rubbed her chin with my cologne before we got out of the blind to admire her first trophy. It was a pretty adult panther measuring about 2½ meters (just over 8 feet) from the muzzle to the end of the tail. Lechi put her arms around my neck and kissed me several times on the cheeks in her joy. Again I was troubled by the contact of her body against mine.

The success of that first hunt had removed all my worry about her possible disappointment in case she missed her target. Her frustration might affect the pleasure she obviously felt in my company. My apprehension had prevented me from enjoying the demands of my senses, which were those of a normal man in the presence of a woman who made him crazy. I thought about the dinner I was going to prepare for her at camp to celebrate our success and help to make our short stay in the jungle unforgettable. It was 6 P.M. when we reached the camp.

She enjoyed the dinner, which included a foie gras, chicken roasted on embers with aromatic Montagnard red rice, and a cucumber salad, preceded by a cocktail I invented and named "Safari," a mixture of Veuve Cliquot champagne and vodka in equal parts, with a few drops of lime juice. Our mutual attraction for each other made us spend a sleepless night that I will not attempt to describe. All the lovers in the world can easily guess how it was.

While we were having our breakfast, K'Sou skinned the panther, taking good care to conserve the fur, and then went to visit the baits again. He came back a few hours later to tell us that the buffalo at the second blind had not been touched; however, the one that had attracted the panther had been visited again during the night.

We got ready in a hurry and went back to the blind. The footprints this time were as big as dinner plates—they must have been made by a huge tiger. Lechi and I again got set up in the blind while the trackers left noisily. They would wait on the far bank of the Cam Ly River, which meandered in the region, and would return to us upon hearing shooting.

Before lying on the blanket, I repeated to Lechi what she must do to avoid missing her trophy: "If the animal faces you, shoot at the base of the neck; if it presents its side, shoot behind the shoulder."

She rehearsed the necessary moves, then everything around us fell silent. I felt the moisture of the jungle creep over my skin, including my hands. Or was it the closeness of Lechi? I glanced at her. Her eyes were closed, but I was sure she was not sleeping. I fixed the ragged ceiling of the blind, and images of our past night together filled my tormented mind. I made the first gesture toward her. She was surely expecting it because she responded immediately. As we entwined with each other, our ardor was interrupted by the noise of breaking bones as a large predator tried to drag the bait away with his powerful jaws.

Lechi, her beautiful naked breasts half hidden by her raven hair that had fallen about her, took aim with the .375. I rapidly put a folded towel between her chin and the gunstock before she fired. Yesterday's scene repeated itself: detonation, recoil, and the falling of leaves around us. But this time it was accompanied by angry growls. I looked quickly through the opening and saw the tiger jumping up and down as if it wanted to get rid of something clinging to its back.

"Lechi, shoot again! Put your bullet in its chest, whether it is facing you or not. Aim well—don't shoot it in the head!"

She obeyed without a word and did what I told her. The tiger stopped its bounding and fell on its side. Its tail whipped the air two or three times; then the animal stopped moving. Again we were wrapped in the silence of the jungle. After a few moments, we drank rum from the flask and then got out, holding hands, to admire the king of the forest.

"You killed a magnificent, fully grown male," I said to Lechi. "Its beard is all white and so thick it looks like a necklace. The beast must measure 3 meters 20 (10½ feet) from its muzzle to the end of its tail, and it must weigh about 250 kilos (550 pounds). This is a magnificent trophy!"

Lechi smiled, but she was not exuberant like the first time. She passed her hand through the fur of the tiger and said pensively, "He was so powerful, so courageous just a few minutes ago, a true king of the jungle. And now he is a dead body that even a weak woman can touch without fear. I am going to call him Désiré (the desired one). He will be my last trophy. I am proud to have accomplished, with your help, what I have always dreamed of doing since childhood. I wanted to be a big-game hunter. But I am sad for having ended the life of such a beautiful creature. If you want, I'll accompany you on your hunts, but I will never kill again, not even a partridge. For you, it's different—it's your job and your life. And you are the most wonderful man I have ever met. You are extraordinary everywhere—with or without a weapon, in a room or in the jungle facing dangerous wild animals."

She kissed me, this time on the lips. My trackers coming back to the blind after the shot arrived during our kiss. K'Sou, the best tracker in the high plateau and my friend from childhood, asked me later with a bantering smile, "Must I continue to visit the bait at the second blind? That buffalo is still whole. It will be eaten maybe tonight or tomorrow."

"K'Sou, my client wants to go back to Da Lat now. But continue your daily visits. I am going to take her back; then I'll return to the camp for a few days to shoot the other *k'liou*."

When Lechi talked about paying me for her safari, I replied, "Are you joking? I am not taking money from a woman I have kissed. The safari is my gift, and the trophies are yours."

"But all the expenses you had . . . it's a lot of money. Allow me to pay at least for the skins."

When I refused, she said, "How are you going to pay for the buffaloes, the construction of the blinds, and the trackers?"

"Don't worry. I still have a whole buffalo at the first blind, and I will pay my expenses with the skins of the tiger I'll shoot. I can also sell their bones to Chinese druggists, who make good medicine with them. Don't worry about anything."

She and I became inseparable. In the foreign diplomatic corps everyone talked about the hunt during which the fascinating sister of the first lady had put on her hunting board not only a tiger and a panther but also the professional hunter formerly well known for his superficial attitude of going from one woman to another.

"Oggeri is hooked this time," they said, seeing us together everywhere—in the city or the jungle. We did not care what people might say. One day the mayor of Da Lat asked me to come to his office, where he warned me against seeing Lechi.

"Don't you realize that this lady is taboo? She is untouchable because she belongs to the ruling family. In addition she is still officially married because Madame Nhu has forbidden divorce in Vietnam. Madame Lechi was divorced in France, but it doesn't count here because of the first lady's Family Law. If you make Madame Nhu angry, bad things could happen to you."

In spite of this warning, Lechi and I continued to see each other. My friends told me that the "terrible lovers," as people called us, and our torrid romance were the subject of everyone's conversation. After several warnings from the mayor, the bell tolled for me. The Home Secretary asked me to come to his office because he had something extremely important to tell me. As soon as he saw me, he said without preamble, "I am sorry, Mr. Oggeri, but you have two weeks to liquidate your business and leave the country."

I could not believe my ears: "Why? What is the reason for this arbitrary order?"

"You are dangerous to this government because of your connections with France's Military Intelligence and the American CIA. You are accused of training the anti-Diem mountain men to shoot with scope-equipped rifles to try to gun down the president or his counselor brother Nhu, who goes hunting sometimes. That's why we have to deport you."

"Do you have any proof of my alleged 'subversive activities'?" I asked.

"We have all the evidence we need."

Fortunately for me, Lechi's parents believed in my innocence. Thanks to their intervention and the important positions they occupied in the government as ambassadors to the United States, I obtained a delay of several months to prepare myself better for a new life in an unknown country.

The hunt with Lechi was a great success for Sladang Safari, and I received many letters from hunters all over the world eager to have me as their guide. I could accept only a few—among them Berry B. Brooks—because I was jailed on 27 September 1962 and then deported to Cambodia on 15 October of the same year.

# Berry B. Brooks and His Passion for Big-Game Hunting

## Chapter 16

My first customer after my hunt with Lechi was William Consley of the Borg-Warner Company in Pennsylvania. After his safari of twenty-eight days, I took him to the airport and he left for the United States, which I conceived of as a different kind of jungle with skyscrapers instead of trees. He was pleased with the results of his hunts, but at the same time a little bitter because he had shot a golden panther, believing it was a giant tiger. In his opinion it was not an important trophy. He called it the "golden cat," not knowing that his golden cat was one of the rarest trophies in the world.

He had shot this trophy at 10 P.M. after having visited the blind earlier that day. Consley had been impressed by the huge footprints left around the bait by a very large tiger and wanted to hunt the animal without delay. He had insisted on waiting alone in the blind, and I reluctantly agreed since he'd told me earlier about his hunting experiences in Assam where he had lain in wait alone for wild beasts.

Noticing my worried expression, he had said, "Don't worry, Etienne, I know the clauses of our contract, and I realize I have to pay for any animal I shoot, whether or not I kill it."

In the blind he had everything he needed within easy reach—his Winchester .375 H&H Magnum loaded with softnose bullets, six-volt headlamp, Thermos of coffee mixed with cognac, a comfortable mattress, and DDT powder to keep the forest parasites away. Night was quickly falling, so after reminding the hunter to lift the wide straw window to ensure a wider angle for night shooting, my guides and I left noisily to make the tiger believe that no one would be there to disturb him when he felt like coming on the bait. That trick was not always successful, however. Sometimes a beast came out of hiding after half an hour and would start eating, but it also sometimes happened that he might come back only the next day—or never, if something about the blind made him suspicious.

At my Jeep more than a mile away, my guides and I had finished a meal and were enjoying a cigarette when we heard the agreed-upon signal: one shot to indicate the animal had come and been shot, a second shot to announce its death. Happily, we raced toward the blind.

I found William seated on a tree trunk, angrily chewing his Montagnard tobacco. When he had arrived in Saigon, he discovered that the suitcase containing his hunting clothes, hunting knife, and favorite chewing tobacco had been lost on the way. My tailor had been able to make four sets of hunting clothes for him the next day before he had to leave for Da Lat. As for the tobacco, he had to be content with the Montagnard brand, which gave off such a bad odor that humans as well as mosquitoes stayed away from the user. The hunter ended up getting so used to it, however, that he asked me to buy two pounds for him to take back to the United States. He intended to chew this "ripe" tobacco at official parties to bother the big bosses of important business companies.

As soon as he saw me he exclaimed, "Etienne, I made a big mistake—I shot too fast. If I had waited a little, I would have realized that it was not a tiger but a smaller cat. I saw only its eyes, which shone in the beam of my lamp. I saw it and shot."

When I saw the animal he had shot, a cat measuring about 1.50 meters (5 feet) in length and weighing about 60 kilos (130 pounds), I said, "That's OK, William. I'll give you another chance for the tiger, and I'll keep this cat for my collection of trophies."

This man who had hunted in India, Africa, Colombia, and Venezuela did not know he had just killed one of the world's most valuable trophies, the golden panther, also called the Temmincki panther. When I explained this to him, his expression changed, and he replied, laughing loudly, "I withdraw what I just said. I still have one day to finish my safari. I'll return to the blind tomorrow, and I'll keep my panther."

I allowed my compassion to dominate my sense of business: "Don't worry, William—if the tiger does not come back, at the end of the hunting season I'll send you a tiger skin with its head mounted. It will be your tiger, the one you would have killed along with this panther."

I felt sorry for this old-looking man with white hair. When he shook my hand on the day of his departure, he had tears in his eyes. He gave me a check for two hundred dollars—"For your *beau geste* (magnanimous gesture)," he said.

After Consley left, two government officials came and handed me a letter: "You are Etienne Oggeri of Sladang Safari, are you not? This is a letter from the ministers of Interior and Tourism."

I took the letter and put it in my pocket. They added hurriedly, "The ministers are waiting for you. We are to take you to the ministry of Interior."

I opened the letter, an urgent invitation. When I arrived at the Ministry of Interior office, I thought I was dreaming. Those two important people, who were known for being impossible to reach, came forward with outstretched hands. They were always busy or absent and could seldom see anyone, even if the person requesting an interview had an important reason for daring to bother them.

After many words of welcome delivered with big smiles, they said—as if sharing an important secret—what I had known for two weeks: "Mr. Oggeri, you will have the honor of guiding in your safaris a man with the reputation of being the best hunter alive, Monsieur Berry Boswell Brooks from Memphis, Tennessee. He has chosen you to be his professional hunter and guide. He wants to reserve you for a twenty-two-day safari, and wishes to have among his trophies a large tiger, a seladang, and a banteng. Please, do everything possible to satisfy him. You'll have all our help. This customer must be pleased because he represents the future of tourism in Vietnam."

"Sir," I replied, "seladang, a word that always impresses foreigners, is only the Indonesian name for gaur. As for the tiger, it's a matter of luck."

They did not seem convinced, so I added, "The tigers in the Lang Bian high plateau are always more impressive than those on the plain. Because of the cold climate of the high region, their fur is thicker, which makes them look bigger than the ones on the plain. However, one can shoot very large tigers in the Krong Pha plain. I have shot several there that were over three meters (almost ten feet) long. As for the banteng and the gaur, the customer will have to decide which one he wants since there is a distance of more than two hundred kilometers (one hundred twenty-five miles) between those two animals. You find the gaur on the high plateau and the banteng in the Krong Pha plain. I have already established the camp for Mr. Brooks at Djiring on the high plateau. Building another one on the plain with different personnel would cost too much. Moreover, twenty-two days would not be long enough for such a safari."

My explanation did not convince the two men who wanted me to accomplish the impossible in order to please Mr. Brooks.

"Mr. Brooks is a multimillionaire," said one of them. "He will pay the extra expenses. Don't forget, Mr. Oggeri, that this unusual customer holds in his hands the future of tourist hunting here. A committee of the Safari Club in Texas has given him the responsibility of evaluating the hunting possibilities of this country. His report to the members of the club will mean either a bright future for tourism in Vietnam or the end of it. Therefore, please do what you can to please him. Doing so would also be in your best interest because you are the only professional hunter who is well known by foreigners."

Their speech amazed me, and it also gave me a slight hope that the government had perhaps decided not to deport me after this last safari. These two secretaries of State might hold in their hands the power to delay my deportation or even cancel it altogether if I made this safari a big success. Taking advantage of their enthusiasm and their promise to make my job easier, I offered some advice about how they could improve the present state of hunting in Vietnam:

"Messieurs, if you want to improve tourist hunting, please make it easier to apply to bring a third weapon and a surplus of ammunition into our country. Those tourists are not arms or ammunition dealers, and they want to enjoy their stay in the jungle. They don't want to be bothered by a lack of ammunition or by the fact that they don't have their shotguns if they want to shoot birds, for example. The province chiefs should also allow professional hunters to have easy access to hunting areas so they can evaluate whether to establish future camps there.

"Another important way to make hunting here more attractive is to tightly control hunting businesses created here. Many hunting amateurs attracted by the prospect of getting a lot of money from foreigners make promises that are impossible to keep, such as giving them a gaur, a black or pink panther, and maybe even a white elephant *on the same safari*. Their safaris always end up causing complaints to the American or Japanese or

French embassy, depending on the nationality of the dissatisfied customer. Such dishonest guides can ruin tourist hunting. My customers are always happy because I try to live up to my reputation as the best professional guide in the country."

On 5 February 1961, Berry B. Brooks landed for the first time in South Vietnam, the still-little-known paradise of hunting. I was his guide, the one he had asked for by name after one of his friends from the State Department had praised me.

I met him as he got off the plane and could see right away by his attitude that my worldwide reputation had made a good impression on him. He grasped my hand firmly while introducing himself and expressing his pleasure to meet me. I replied by saying how honored and proud I was to have him as my client. Perhaps he did not fully understand what I'd said because of my strong French accent, and, as for me, I could barely understand him with his American southern accent.

After putting his luggage in my Land Rover, we went to the Ministry of Tourism to retrieve his weapons and get his permits. We met the minister, who asked me to introduce Berry to him. With a large smile, he thanked the famous visitor for honoring South Vietnam by coming for a safari, and wished him good luck. Berry laughed, tapped my shoulder, and replied, "I don't need luck—my luck is having him as my guide."

I suggested that he rest that night in Saigon. In the morning my assistant would take him to the plane for Da Lat. He refused, preferring to leave immediately with me in my car and travel by night. He was impatient to immerse himself in the untamed parts of the country as soon as possible. He hoped to see wild animals alongside the roads, as he had in Africa. I explained to him that it was rare to see a tiger or panther on the edge of the jungle. Sometimes, but not often, one could see a sambar deer or a wild boar.

We reached Da Lat in the evening. I took him to the Lang Bian Palace, the city's most luxurious hotel, and invited him for dinner. I wanted him to meet my friend Lechi. Berry was very impressed with her beauty when she arrived in the traditional *ao dai*, a pink dress tightly fitted at the waist but slit on the sides so that the lightest breeze lifted the panels, revealing black satin pants. He asked her to order for him three similar dresses but of different colors: "One like yours, and the other two in your choice of colors," he said.

He also wanted hunting uniforms like mine since he found them elegant, simple, and light. He gave Lechi his measurements and his wife's. She assured him they would be ready when he left for home.

After dinner we invited him to have coffee at Lechi's house and to view our trophy room, which was remarkable not only for the number of animal skins and horns but also for the profusion of various species of orchids that I had brought from the jungle for her. While drinking his jasmine tea, Berry asked me why I collected several trophies of the same kind.

"These trophies belong to both Lechi and me. She keeps hers, but I sell mine. When a customer misses his target, he often wants to buy a similar trophy. Therefore, I hunt during the monsoon season and manage to fill the room with trophies from which my customers can choose."

Very interested in my explanation, Berry said, "If I miss my tiger—I already have two but they are not records—I want one like these."

He especially admired two beautiful tiger skins, each measuring 3.25 meters (10½ feet). I told him that a hunter did not often have the opportunity to shoot such outstanding animals but that I was in a different situation since I was constantly in the jungle and around wild beasts at least three hundred days a year. So, I sometimes shot such animals, but out of any ten tigers that I killed or helped a customer to kill, only two would be longer than 3 meters (almost 10 feet); the others would tape between 2.6 and 2.9 meters (8½ to 9½ feet). I added, "The unlucky customer who misses his animal usually does not mind if the one he can buy is small. He thinks: 'Big or small, a tiger is still a tiger.'"

"I usually kill my trophies myself," said Berry. "I always try for records, but this hunt is a little special. I am hunting for the Asiatic Hall of the Memphis Museum of Natural History, which I have created. So I want a few difficult-to-find animals, and I am especially looking for record trophies. If I cannot get a ten-foot tiger this time, I will buy one of these two. I'll agree with your price."

I nodded in agreement, but it occurred to me as he was talking that even the most famous hunters needed a professional guide to help them. Most wealthy hunters—whether they came from the United States, France, or Italy—received praises for the trophies they brought back, but these people seldom mention their guides or trackers. It was as if they had done everything by themselves—tracked, shot, and skinned their trophies—and we, the professional guides, had merely followed along to provide the local color. They, however, were the amateurs of the hunt, the way others fished or played golf. They had a passion for it but had not assimilated it totally the way the professional hunter had. Their social status and wealth allowed them to go on two or three safaris a year, and the media praised them for the trophies they brought back. However, I wondered what would become of them should they find themselves in the middle of the jungle, armed with their best guns but lacking in the survival skills that the presence of a professional afforded them.

Often I would allow myself to have some secret fun at the hunter's expense. For example, I would purposely follow gaur tracks that I knew were three or four days old because I could see spider nets and wilted grass in the bottom. My customers, the great hunters who had said they knew how to read the footprints of any animal, would follow me without question, convinced they were hot on the quarry's track. After a few minutes of this game, I would take them back in the right direction.

I saw other great hunters turn their backs and almost run away when they got within thirty feet of an elephant or a gaur. I had to grab hold of their shirts to stop them, and then I would snap: "It's in front of you. Aim and shoot!"

Still others missed a tiger from just twenty meters (sixty-five feet) because the animal had glared at them with its amber eyes and fear had grabbed them and taken hold. A few others simply told me, "I am here to rest. Please go and hunt for me. I am interested only in the trophies." I did not ask them why they did not buy stuffed animals from the taxidermist. I understood that they needed to impress people by telling them they had spent three weeks in the middle of the dangerous jungle.

To me the real hunter was the one who seldom talked about his trophies. He would mention his records only if asked by someone genuinely interested in his hunts or to a prospective buyer, should he decide to sell his trophies. Many such men, however, lived on the edge of the law and, thus, shunned publicity.

We left Da Lat early the next morning, Berry comfortably seated in my Land Rover while I drove. My Willys Jeep and 6x6 Dodge followed with the food supply, the refrigerator, and the wine and liquor cabinet. My camp on the bank of the Da Dung River in the Kinda region was ready, with my staff of servants, cooks, trackers, tanners, porters, and guides waiting.

I had also hired two men to assure Berry B. Brooks's safety. One, a tea-plantation owner named Aimé Plas, was a marksman and the son of a great hunter well known to American tourists in the years 1930–1945. Another, René Fournier, operated a plantation of pine trees grown for their resin in the Da Nhim region, forty-five kilometers (twenty-eight miles) from our camp. My worry about Berry Brooks's safety resulted from two well-known facts: Some of the people in the area were infamous poachers, even though they were not officially allowed to have guns, and, even more importantly, the Viet Cong had started to circulate in the area.

My big fear was the Viet Cong might be tempted to kidnap Berry for ransom. If that had happened, the South Vietnamese government would almost certainly accuse me of selling my American customer to the Viet Cong. I walked a delicate balance. Ngo's government was corrupt, so I would end up the scapegoat if something happened to my client. On the other hand, the Viet Cong were not interested in the French and, by extension, in me, but they were very interested in bringing down the corrupt government of Ngo and would cause as much trouble as possible to reach that goal. Certainly, kidnapping an influential, wealthy American would cause great distress in high places in Saigon.

The two bodyguards had cost me a lot. Theirs was a harsh life with an uncertain future, and landing a lucrative job was a unique opportunity for them. I would not have needed them, however, if Berry had agreed to wait comfortably in a hotel in Djiring until a tiger came on the bait. But, he had refused to stay behind. This intrepid hunter said to me, "I hunted in Kenya, and the Mau Mau never frightened me." I was about to tell him that there was a big difference between the Mau Mau and the Viet Cong, but I changed my mind. I have always believed in avoiding sterile discussions.

Berry was favorably impressed by my camp, made with braided bamboo and *tranh*, a long reed that was better than straw for the roof. The living area for the client and the professional guides included three bedrooms and a large, open middle area that served as the dining room. Well away from the main camp was a roofless bathing room that included a system for either a cold or hot shower. Fifty feet from the camp was the kitchen, next to a hut for use by the native personnel. A path led out through the forest to the latrine, an enclosure with a normal seat above a deep pit that was treated with quicklime.

The area was sprinkled with DDT powder every three days while we were hunting. This system effectively annihilated all insects, noxious or not. Twice, after returning from the jungle, I had been diagnosed with typhus, which the doctor had attributed to tick bites. So before each hunt in areas infested by ticks and fleas, I would sprinkle my body with DDT powder. It was a long time ago, and back then we did not know the harmful effects of DDT or that it could cause cancer.

It was almost lunchtime. My chef, Anh Nam, served us some before-meal drinks with appetizers. Since this was the customer's first food at the camp, I took the opportunity to officially welcome him—with the help of a bottle of Veuve Cliquot brut champagne, cooled in the river that ran in front of the camp. We used the river to refrigerate our reserve of wines, sodas, and canned food, and the chefs kept their vegetables fresh by planting them in the wet sand of the riverbank. Berry could not help telling me how impressed he was by the overall atmosphere of my Sladang Safari organization.

"It's even more impressive than a safari in the Hemingway style," he exclaimed.

Plas and René, my guides and bodyguards, left us after finishing their champagne. Two days before the customer's arrival, Plas had killed two sambar and placed the baits near blinds twelve kilometers (seven and a half miles) from the camp on the Kinda trail, which was often visited by tigers. He and René wanted to check the baits. While waiting for their return, we had lunch.

In spite of my French accent and Berry's southern U.S. drawl, we managed to understand each other. He told me about his safaris in Assam and Kashmir, and I told him about my hunting areas of R'Pouma Klong, Krong Pha, Kinda, Djiring, and Cagne. At one point after lunch, Berry asked whether I had any whiskey, which he liked to drink with soda. I handed him a bottle of Black and White, but the expression on his face told me he did not care for that brand.

"Don't you have Johnny Walker, Black Label, or Chivas?" he asked.

"No. Under this new regime we don't have much choice as far as wines and liquor are concerned. Imports of liquor are minimal. Only the American PX sells those famous brands, and on the local market Black and White is the best."

"I guess I will have to adopt the attitude of the unlucky customers who buy a tiger skin from you and say, 'Large or small, it's still a tiger.' Whether Black and White or Chivas, it's still whiskey," Berry said, laughing.

I had the impression he was making fun of me. I looked at his face, all wrinkled by his outburst of mirth, and replied in French with a smile, "*Eh, oui, faute de grives on se contente de merles* (half a loaf is better than no bread). Do you know that French proverb?"

He shook his head and answered in French (I'm translating here): "Is that French? It's too deep for a cotton merchant from Tennessee."

He must have learned that sentence recently because he said it in my language without a mistake. I had to admit it was very appropriate.

Then he added in English, "That's all I can say in your language."

About that point the guides returned, and the news they brought back was not good: The tiger had not come to the bait. To keep Berry busy I took him in my Willys with the top down to shoot pheasants, francolins, and wild chickens on the trails leading to various Montagnard villages in the region. He asked whether I had a shotgun. I said I had one but had only buckshot to put in it. That illegal weapon was for the protection of the camp. I shot my small game with a .22 Long Rifle Mauser Oberndorf made in 1910, a marvel of precision with five bullet loaders.

"You must shoot very well," Berry said. "But what do you do when the birds fly?"

"I shoot them then, too, but with less satisfying results. My grandfather, who was building the railroad, the tunnels, and the road that went from Nha Trang to Ban Me Thuot, taught me how to shoot when I was five, and I would shoot turtledoves that flew over our bungalow in the Ro Thon Pass. Every evening the pigeons would fly back over our camp, and I would hide myself in the bamboo with a 6mm Bosquette. The closest birds were twenty feet away. I would shoot several in the evening using the 6mm."

Berry seemed to admire what I told him about my ability as a marksman. I explained that I preferred to shoot birds with a shotgun and No. 6 or 8 birdshot, which did not destroy meat like the high-speed .22 Long Rifle bullet. Unfortunately, the roar of the shotgun made the game suspicious, especially tigers that might be prowling nearby.

When we still had not drawn in a tiger on the second day, I decided to put Berry on the tracks of a solitary gaur, seen five kilometers (three miles) from camp by one of my trackers on his way back to his village. The animal was going toward the *dâtches* (salt licks) in the region of Bross Deur. With a little luck the hunters would see him in the afternoon.

Berry and his two guides/bodyguards left the camp at 6:30 A.M. accompanied by two trackers and one porter carrying food. Plas told me later that after three hours of tracking amid the bamboo and thornbushes bordering the Da Dung River, they spotted the lone gaur, which presented its left side to them at a range of forty meters (one hundred thirty feet). Its dark and powerful body stood out against a background of bushes.

Berry aimed and shot just as the gaur got the scent of the hunters, and the animal bolted away. The gaur stumbled under the impact of the bullet but continued its escape. René, armed with my .30-06 Garand, fired two solid bullets in rapid succession at the same time Plas fired my 10.75x68 Francotte. The huge animal stopped, fell on its knees, lifted its muzzle toward the sky, uttered a sad bellow, then dropped. Berry rushed toward the beast and saw a huge hole in the belly, another in the thigh, and two small holes behind the head toward the cervical vertebrae. All three shooters had hit the target, which seemed to bother Berry a lot. He came back to René and Plas and told them not to dismember the animal right away.

"I'll return with Etienne and the porters. After the pictures are taken, the men will cut up the beast according to Etienne's instructions."

In spite of the good results of the expedition, I noticed that my customer was ill humored back at the camp. I asked Plas for the details of the last moments of the hunt.

"We all fired. However, in my opinion it was the two bullets from the .30-06 fired by René that stopped the gaur. I shot at his rear, hoping to break his hip with my solid, but he kept going. Berry's bullet caused a lot of damage in the belly and destroyed the liver, lungs, and bowels, but it did not touch the heart because the gaur still had the strength to run both rapidly and powerfully. You know how strong those giants are. The animal would still have been able to cover ground, and in that region of old fields it would have been very dangerous to track a wounded gaur. I did not want to be in that situation!"

During dinner Berry asked me to go with him the next day to see the gaur. He wanted to take pictures and especially get my opinion on which bullet had killed the gaur—meaning who was responsible for getting the trophy. I saw that this question really bothered him.

After a complete autopsy of the animal, I found out that Berry's bullet had mushroomed well and devastated stomach, liver, and kidneys. The heart had not been touched (I kept it for a stew with wine). I removed the two 7mm .30-06 solids from the cervical vertebrae and the big 10.75 projectile from the belly. The 10.75 had broken the hip, gone through the muscles of the thigh, and ended up in the bowels. That gaur had been mortally wounded. Plas was right, however; it would still have covered a lot of distance in thick thornbushes—exactly the kind of cover a hunter with common sense dreads going through.

We took a thigh, two fillets, and the heart back to my chefs. The remaining meat was for the trackers' village. The head, skin, and two feet were part of the trophy.

In spite of the abundant champagne accompanying it, the dinner lacked cheerfulness. Berry was in a bad mood and did not talk. Plas and René put an end to his silence by inviting him to come with them to the village where the chief was waiting for us with a jar of corn alcohol. He refused with haughtiness, not realizing that his refusal could offend the sensitive Montagnards, who might then refuse to come back and help with the hunting. To offset the bad impression caused by Berry's attitude, I called to my friends and the trackers, who were leaving without saying a word, and offered them a carton of Bastos cigarettes and two bottles of pastis.

"Mr. Brooks does not feel well," I explained, "but I will come later."

As I finished my glass of champagne, Berry asked me point-blank, "Etienne, do you sincerely believe that my bullet alone could have killed that gaur?"

"Certainly, Berry. Although your bullet did not hit the vital points, it caused considerable damage. The animal could not have run more than three hundred meters (one thousand feet). René's two solids only gave him the coup de grace, which stopped him dead. This gaur belongs to you alone, Berry, and there is no doubt in my mind that you are responsible for this fine trophy."

He relaxed, replying with a happy smile, "You should have been an ambassador instead of a hunter."

"I have to go to the village of Ko Yan," I told him, "to get some information about the passage of a herd of elephants the villagers saw yesterday. It's on the Kinda trail, where I have set my tiger blinds. Would you like to come with me?"

Berry said he was not interested in elephants—they were small compared to the ones in Africa. So I left alone. The villagers told me the herd had gone toward the river Dam Rong, more than eighty kilometers (fifty miles) from Kinda. They also informed me that a tiger had come to a bait. I returned immediately to the camp to tell Berry the good news.

George, a planter in the Kinda area, was waiting there to let me know that René had decided to quit. "He doesn't want to continue working for you. He wants to go home and asks whether you can pay him. He is waiting for me at the village and would appreciate if you could give me his salary. I am going to give him a ride to Djiring, where he will take a taxi home. He apologizes for letting you down, but he hopes you'll understand his decision. Now you better go take care of Berry. I'll explain things in detail later when you are back. Nothing very alarming."

I told Berry that a bait had been visited by a tiger. He was impatient to go to the blind and wasn't hungry for lunch. I instructed my chef to prepare a snack and some coffee for him to take to the blind.

It was 1 P.M. when we arrived at the blind. Studying the tiger's footprints revealed that it was a young male that would not measure over 2.8 meters (9 feet). I told Berry about my discovery, and he did not seem enthusiastic about this animal. But I said, "Who knows? Maybe a big tiger will come and drive away the small one. Go into the blind and try your luck. Sometimes the unexpected happens in the jungle. Don't lose hope."

He remained undecided, so I added with a laugh, "Big or small, a tiger is still a tiger!"

He finally entered the blind, and we left him alone. He had already killed two tigers in Bengal and Assam and did not want my help. I reminded him of what he should do if the beast came at night: Lift the windowpane to get a better view of the target, then shoot two times to announce its death.

Then my trackers and I left noisily. We were drinking cold beer and smoking when we heard a rifle roar. Berry had shot his tiger! A second shot told us the animal was dead! It was five in the afternoon.

Full of anticipation, we rushed in my Jeep to the blind. From afar I could see anger on my client's face. He could not understand why he had missed his tiger from a distance of twenty meters (sixty-five feet). I carefully inspected the bait and, with my trackers' help, started to look for traces of blood. Some two hundred yards from the blind I found substantial traces of thick red blood, which had not come from a wound in the belly. The tiger had been hit, but where? Perhaps in the thighs?

I continued to follow the blood trail and a hundred yards farther I saw the animal limping away on three legs. It saw our group and moved away without showing any aggressiveness. I did not have time to return and tell Berry, who had remained at the blind to relieve his upset stomach behind a bush. I aimed at the poor handicapped cat, and a solid from my .375 Francotte ended its short life.

From muzzle to tip of tail, the tiger measured 2.9 meters (9½ feet). I said jokingly to Berry, "If you pull a little on the skin, it will stretch to 10 feet—the length you wanted. Are you pleased?"

"Yes and no," he answered. "Yes for the size of the tiger. Of course, I would have preferred one of 11½ feet. I'll try again next year. What bothers me is my shooting. I wonder whether I am having problems with my eyes or my age. It seems I no longer shoot like I did before."

"Well," I said, "you are no longer young, but you still shoot very well. Judging by what I saw from your hits on the gaur, you aimed at the left shoulder, hoping to hit the heart, but you hit the belly. This means you were off by 60 centimeters (about 23 inches) at a distance of 30 meters (100 feet). Now you just shot a tiger from a distance of 20 meters (65 feet). You aimed at the base of the neck since the animal was facing you, and your bullet hit the left foot that it had placed on the bait animal's chest, which is a deviation of 60 centimeters (23 inches) again. I believe there is nothing wrong with your eyes. It's your scope that needs to be zeroed. Let's test it right away before we have another fiasco."

To my surprise, he categorically refused my suggestion. "My weapons are the best quality, my scopes were made in Germany, and the mount was made by a master of German gunnery. Nothing can be wrong with the mounting system, which is foolproof. If I miss my target once again, we'll see."

"If I were you, Berry, I would not wait until then. Next time you could be facing a charge, or maybe you'll have a chance at the largest white tiger you have ever seen and you'll miss it. Think it over. You still have a few days left, and there is one untouched bait."

I was annoyed when he told me his weapons were the best in the world. I said to myself that I would not have traded one of my Francottes mounted on a Mauser Oberndorf Magnum breech with double square bridge for his entire collection. Although the impact of a .460 or a .378 is very powerful, the killing power of the .416, .404, or .505 is far better. However, everyone to his own taste. Berry had a weakness for new rifles with very expensive ammunition.

Since I was not a fanatic about those bazookas, I had early on chosen the .404 and 10.75 with an octagonal barrel. Because of the difficulty of finding .404 ammunition, however, I had switched that gun for a .375 H&H and my old 10.75 with the octagonal barrel. With those calibers I could shoot any animal from the muntjac to the elephant without any problem. Naturally, it was necessary to place the bullet in a vital place and not in the belly.

Berry wanted to watch the skinning of the tiger. So he went off, and I took advantage of his absence to ask George why René had quit so suddenly. He explained with some embarrassment that René could easily see that Berry was angry with him for having shot at the gaur. The client apparently wanted to have all the credit for his trophy.

George told me, "Mr. Brooks openly criticized both René and Plas in front of them as he believes they don't speak enough English to understand him."

"What did Mr. Brooks say?" I asked.

"Mr. Brooks said, 'They are not suitable as guides, and Etienne had better get rid of them. They spend their time drinking and playing cards when he is not there. Anyway, I'll tell him myself about that.'"

"René also noticed," George added, "that Berry never shook hands with him or talked to him, though he behaved differently with Plas, certainly because Plas is white. René feels that your customer treated him like trash because he is half black. (His mother was from Martinique.) Everyone knows about the Americans' racial discrimination against black people. So René feels offended. He didn't want to cause you any problems, so he prefers to leave. He is now at the village waiting for me to give him a ride to Djiring. He said he would appreciate if you could give him his salary. I'll bring it to him with his bag when I leave in one hour."

I was very disturbed by this incident between my client and my friend. René had even proposed patrolling at night to assure Brooks's safety. He had also volunteered to get information about Viet Cong in the area. Though the guerrillas did not attack French citizens, René was nonetheless risking his life because they might have executed him as an example to those who were thinking about collaborating with the Americans. My first reaction was indignation against Berry Brooks for his racism.

After a night of reflection, I decided to let it go and only talk about it if my client said something. I would then tell him that René had left suddenly because of family problems. I thought it unnecessary to quarrel with Berry. However, I felt very disappointed by his attitude. The sympathy I had felt for him at the beginning of the safari switched to irritation. Then I remembered that the French also had been guilty of racial discrimination against the natives. It was fortunate that the French had finally risen above that stupid arrogance!

Plas, who had gone to check on the last bait, came back to tell us that it had been touched by a big animal, but in spite of his hunting experience, he was unsure what kind of beast it was. The grass-covered ground did not reveal whether a tiger, a panther, or wild boars had come to devour the deer.

Berry and I visited the site, and I, too, was unable to read the footprints. Berry was sure it was a big tiger because of the large opening made by its passage through the tall *tranh* grass. This time he asked me to stay with him.

"I might need your help if the shooting takes place in the dark," he said. "Since it is already late, the animal will probably not come until night."

We installed ourselves comfortably on our mattress with coffee, headlamps, and guns within reach. I went over with Berry the moves he would need to make to be successful. After a short while his loud snoring troubled the silence. I broke a twig from the wall of the blind and lightly passed it along his ear. The snoring stopped immediately. Less than fifteen minutes later I heard a sound like the stamping of an elephant in the tall grass. The noise drew nearer. I woke Berry, handed him his .378 with scope, and signaled to him to aim toward the bait. Since he could not see anything, I whispered in his ear, "Be ready to shoot."

I turned on the light. Everything seemed dark at the bait, but something large was standing next to the deer carcass, trying to tear it up. I finally recognized the monster as a Tibetan bear, the famous Asiatic giant with its yellow "necklace." On its hind legs it stood about 2.15 meters (7 feet) tall, and would weigh more than 250 kilos (550 pounds). It was really a handsome specimen. It was facing us, so we could see its yellow necklace and red mouth, which was holding a chunk of putrefied meat.

Berry fired. The thunderous explosion temporarily deafened us, and a flash of light similar to the one produced by a flame-thrower during the war in the Pacific blinded us. The bear fell on all fours and rapidly disappeared in the tall grass, heading for dense forest. My customer was stunned, realizing he had again missed an easy target. It was too late for either of us to shoot again. We got out of the blind to join Plas, who had come after hearing the shot. He and the trackers immediately started their search for traces of blood, but Berry stopped them.

"It's not necessary—I missed it," he said. "I aimed at the base of the neck. Its chest was at least forty inches wide, and it was facing me. In Etienne's headlight I saw it as clearly as if in full daylight. I couldn't have missed, but I did. I am getting old and I believe my eyes are playing tricks on me."

I told him again that his scope was not working correctly. We decided then to test it the next day.

After breakfast Berry tested his weapons. He had no problems with his .300 Weatherby, but with his .378 he was shooting 60 centimeters (23 inches) to the right and 40 centimeters (15 inches) high. The sighting-in exercise restored his cheerfulness: He was still the greatest hunter of all, the famous marksman of worldwide reputation. He told me how sorry he felt for not listening to me about his scope earlier.

It was the end of his twenty-two-day safari. We returned to Da Lat, where his second tiger was waiting for him in my trophy room. He bought it for two hundred dollars, which is the price I usually sold them for in Vietnam. I had no idea about the prices of tiger skins in America. Lechi advised me to learn the price of trophies in the United States before selling my tiger so cheap, but I did not listen to her. Berry did not tell me the value of a tiger skin in America, but he could not help saying, "Etienne, you are a good guide, a great hunter, but a bad businessman."

He returned to the United States pleased with his safari. He had in his luggage for his museum in Memphis two striped cats, one of which was unusually big, and a pair of gaur horns spreading fully 1 meter (39 inches) between their widest points and, therefore, a trophy superior to the one exhibited at the museum of Bombay.

I found out later that my tiger of 3.15 meters (10.3 feet), tanned by Jonas Bros. with all its claws and with whiskers on its mounted head, was worth $15,000 in 1963 in the United States. I was sorry I hadn't listened to Lechi—all the more so since she did not find it necessary to say to me, "I told you."

Later I wrote to Berry to tell him that the second gaur, which he had shot all by himself some time after the first one, had been found by George. Its horns, eaten by termites, had a spread of 1.5 meters. My letter remained unanswered. For this great hunter, his safari in Vietnam was apparently a thing of the past and he was no longer interested in it. Yet he had hired me for another safari in 1962, a two-month trip for himself and a friend. They wanted, among other trophies, the three bovines of South Vietnam and a kouprey from Cambodia. Other hunters, too, had made reservations to have me as their guide until 1963. Alas, however, the knell had rung for me.

A few days after the end of Berry's safari, I was again notified that I was being expelled from Vietnam—the first French citizen singled out for deportation. The whole population knew about the arbitrary decree of expulsion against me, for I had become the companion of Lechi, the sister of the first lady, Madame Nhu. That woman had launched a campaign of morality to mask her own scandalous conduct with the various ambassadors to Vietnam. Now she needed to make a point that nobody was above her laws, not even the members of her own family. Only her husband's brothers, who were interested not in women but in money, could dig in the country's coffers without being punished.

A few days after Brooks's safari, I had to return all my guns and my passport to the government of South Vietnam. I was once more notified of my expulsion, but given an extension of thirteen months to put my affairs in order. During that delay, Lechi and I never lost the hope that Madame Nhu would change her mind about my deportation and perhaps just forget us since we did not meddle in politics. We were mistaken. As the fateful date approached, she became more hateful. Lechi's mother had to fly to Vietnam to rescue her daughter from her sister's persecution. But that is another long story for a book I might write someday.

# Why I Gave Up Hunting

## Chapter 17

The events related in this chapter took place a few months before my safari with Berry Brooks.

It was the end of my last campaign for ivory with my loyal guide K'Sou near the village of Talou at the foot of the Bidup Mountain in the zone of Krong Pha. That area had the reputation of being crowded with elephants, but it was too far from the Da Lat–Nha Trang highway, so very few people knew about that paradise of big game.

After five weeks of walking behind elephants, I had succeeded in shooting three beautiful trophies. I decided to follow the trail of the big animals once more in the hope of getting a big tusker to conclude that hunt. We planned to leave our camp the next day.

K'Sou and my two other guides were studying numerous tracks when they were interrupted by a group of Montagnards from a village on the mountainside. When K'Sou told them we were pursuing a herd of elephants, the leader of the villagers informed us they had seen, that same morning, a large group of the animals about six miles from where we were, heading toward the sacred mountain. Earlier the men had seen other, smaller herds that seemed to be going in the same direction.

After a few minutes of animated conversation with them, K'Sou said to me, "I don't believe they are exaggerating, Ông Tienne. This village chief seems serious. He said he has even seen several big tuskers among all those animals—several hundred of them, he said. It's the first time in his life he has seen such a gathering."

We discussed this for a little while. Since my guide seemed to believe the veracity of the information, we went back to our camp to pack enough food and equipment for a pursuit of two or three days. I gathered three more guides from the area, and then we were off.

During our lunch I watched K'Sou. He and the others firmly believed in that incredible migration. K'Sou was well aware of the jungle inhabitants' tendency to exaggerate when telling a story, but this time he believed them. As for me, the more I thought about the mass exodus, the less I believed it could happen.

The tracks we had seen in the morning showed a small herd walking in the direction of the mountain. A story told by my old friend Charles, nicknamed Charlot, came back to my mind. Charlot had a plantation in Djiring, but he was also well known as a hunter. He had taught me a lot about the art of big-game hunting. One evening, as we talked around our fire during a hunt near Dông Mé, Charlot started a strange story about the migration of elephants. We had drunk a lot to celebrate the first elephant of our campaign, and Charlot was eloquent.

He was hunting near Bryan Mountain in Djiring when he saw a large herd, the largest in his life. He followed it and realized that other, smaller herds were joining it. Eventually the gathering took the trail to the Gia Lam Pass, heading in the direction of Phan Thiet. He was not equipped for a long pursuit, so he returned home to get an extra rifle and ammunition, as well as enough food for several days, and then left with a group of trackers and bearers. As they headed toward the Gia Lam pass, Charlot dreamed of the beautiful tusks he would bring back from that expedition.

The next day, he caught up with the rear of the herd along the River Song Luy. The animals were walking slowly but seemed to have a precise destination in mind. Charlot followed them. He saw very big tuskers but could not shoot since they were still too far away. Late in the afternoon he reached a high place from which he could see the entire impressive cortege moving along. I had never known my friend to exaggerate when telling a hunting story (he did so only when describing the charms of his latest "bird of paradise," as he called the prostitutes). The herd—consisting of more than a hundred beasts—was between two hills. He did not dare to approach close enough to shoot but continued to follow. At dusk he was able to kill two bulls. The herd panicked and fled, sounding almost like a hurricane as they shattered bamboo branches and caused avalanches of rocks.

Charlot and his men camped near the two dead elephants and took advantage of that rest period to extract the tusks. From time to time they heard shrill trumpeting in the distance, then everything went silent. Early the next morning they were again on the herd's trail, hoping to get a few more trophies. They walked for two days paralleling the Rivers Song Luy and Song Mao, but could not catch up with the elephants—they had disappeared. The only trace of their passage was visible in a forest of *bang-lang*, where the ground was packed down and leveled. It looked like a dance floor. What unbelievable activity had they performed there? Charlot decided they had gathered there to dance in the new moon.

I had never seen such a "dance floor" in the forest. The old Montagnards, however, affirm that elephants gather once every twenty years to dance together for one evening. I am inclined to believe them. The people of the jungles know and see many things that escape the rest of us.

Now, back to my own hunt: When I entered the forest of giant bamboo, I saw tracks made recently by several herds in their march to join the main group. I could not say exactly how many were in that main band, but I can affirm I had never seen so many elephants together. When we stopped to camp for the night, I heard their trumpeting, as well as the noise of bamboo branches being broken and crushed. The herds were eating. I would have to wait until morning to assess wind direction and try a prudent approach.

Approaching a herd of that size is very dangerous. Elephants of all ages—bulls, mothers, and babies—were circulating in that ocean of bamboo, and if the wind changed direction or something else unexpected happened, they would all flee in panic. Hunters call this rushing of the monsters a "collective charge." With their trunks extended they try to find out the source of the danger, and sometimes they flee right toward the hunter.

I wanted to avoid provoking such a collective panic. Looking for adult bulls would take time, but I wanted to shoot big tuskers, not vindictive young bodyguards. I hid behind a large bush and watched. Soon I saw a big male breaking young clumps of bamboo. His long tusks and huge head were visible over the bushes, appearing and disappearing at regular intervals. A little later another beast joined him. It was a young bull that I categorized as a "trouble-maker not suitable for a shot."

He seemed nervous as he sniffed the big tusker, and raised his radarlike trunk that looked like a monstrous leech full of blood. Slowly he came toward me. Without hesitation I fired at the big male, which seemed about to follow his young protector. My .404 solid hit him between the eyes and he collapsed in a mass. His young companion passed me like a tank, so close that I saw his yellow eyes. He was panicked but furious. He ran about sixty feet, then returned to his fallen companion and walked around him two or three times. Trumpeting, he tried to move the old bull. When he realized that he was powerless to help, he ran away trumpeting with rage, his screams resounding through the whole forest.

I stayed motionless, watching the herd, which moved in a file in front of me at about thirty feet. One magnificent male was walking between two young bulls, seemingly his bodyguards. His short but massive tusks had a magnificent patina—shiny and golden. I did not hesitate one second, firing into the cavity of his ear. He fell while the herd began running. K'Sou and I approached him.

My guide caressed the tusks, looked at me, and said, "Ông Tienne, these tusks are not long, but I believe you have never obtained a more beautiful pair except the one on the rogue of Ratanakiri. They are at least 1.5 meters (5 feet) long and must weigh over 40 kilos (88 pounds)."

We saw other bulls, but they were young. I was very pleased with my trophies and prepared for our return to camp. Because we would have to cross an immense savanna, I decided to take another way, which led through a deep forest of *bang-lang* with many clearings in it. I went across the first clearing and had started to climb a little brushy slope when a small group of elephants came out of some bushes. There were two young bulls and two or three big females with young. I did not shoot, and they continued on their way.

The young bulls, however, retraced their steps, then disappeared behind a big clump of bamboo. Soon they emerged from the cover, flanking an old bull. He had only one tusk of an unusual whiteness. The two bodyguards, with precise and well-synchronized movements, encouraged the patriarch to catch up with the herd. I aimed at the old male and shot him as he was running. He fell, got up, and, with the help of his two protectors, succeeded in escaping on shaky legs, zigzagging from side to side. I had hit him but not well enough to anchor him.

K'Sou and I took the time to smoke a cigarette and then began the pursuit. We had gone a mile or so—accompanied by the angry trumpeting of adult beasts, the plaintive cries of panicked babies, and the noise of branches being crushed—when the forest became silent. We followed the tracks and soon found a group of elephants in the process of burying their dead one. Females and young males were trying to cover the old bull with dirt and branches.

I took my little U.S. M1 carbine from one of my men and shot five or six rounds in the air to make the herd run away. After they disappeared, we admired the single tusk, which was long and white but not heavy. I decided to end our pursuit.

K'Sou and a bearer had started to remove the tusk when an old female rushed out of a bush. I saw immediately she was old—her ears and forehead were a pinkish color and covered with brown spots. She flattened her ears against her neck, raised her trunk, and ran straight at me. I had promised myself never to shoot at a cow elephant but rather to avoid her as best I could. That is what I did now, but she was on me in a few steps as I was running away. I felt her trunk seize the bottom of my pants. At the same moment a powerful blast reverberated right over my head. My brave guide and friend K'Sou, armed with my .404, stopped her dead in her tracks as he saw me about to be crushed.

I was saddened by her death, and I started to reproach my guide for killing a female. He explained, "She was two steps behind you. Twice she whipped her trunk at your head but missed you. She was catching you by your pants when I shot."

We were looking at her body when I noticed milk dripping from her two breasts . . . this surely must mean she had a baby. At that moment a miniature elephant rushed out from the bush and charged us, flattening his ears against his neck and raising his little trunk, his yellow eyes full of panic and fury. He was very young, black, and still had a lot of hair on his body. He ran straight at K'Sou, trumpeting in a high-pitched tone and whipping his back with his trunk. K'Sou turned around once and fell on the ground—to the great hilarity of the bearers. The little orphan charged us repeatedly, running at us, stopping, then charging again.

We played with him until the moment his charge took him in front of his mother's body. He trembled, hesitated, stepped back, his trunk darting in front of him like a snake. Several times he came back and sniffed the body. When he was sure it was his mother, he smelled her, tried to move her away, and put his trunk into her ears. He sniffed her mouth, dipping his trunk inside. He caressed her, squalling plaintively. His eyes, full of anger and hatred a moment before, were now full of tears. That little elephant was crying like a human baby. He screamed, coughed, and smelled the blood flowing from her wound. With his little shoulder he tried to move her away. Then he lay down between her legs and sucked thirstily on her breasts. Drinking her milk seemed to help him forget his misery, and he fell asleep against her still-hot body.

I felt sick with disgust and regret. I spread my blanket on the ground, lay down on it, and slept while my bearers continued to extract the bull's tusk. In my sleep I felt a warm breath on my chest and had the impression that someone was pulling on my shirt. I woke up with a start and saw that the baby elephant was trying to remove my shirt. His eyes, round and yellow and bordered with long eyelashes, seemed sad.

He was adorable. He had a nearly bald head with a little tuft of hair on top. My own son at his birth was not cuter than this one. Even he had not moved me the way this little animal did. I extended my hand to him. With his trunk he smelled it without showing any sign of animosity. I was alive and warm while his mother's body was becoming cold. His instinct had chosen me. When one of my bearers came in our direction, the little one moved away, then stopped to look at the man and then at me. He did not know whether he could trust us. He went back to his mother and began to drink her milk again.

A few meters away from me a bamboo bush suddenly burst into flames, which spread out very rapidly, catching little branches everywhere. That savanna, covered with dry grass and bushes, soon became an inferno. One of my bearers had fired up a cigarette and thrown away his still-lit match, which was almost like dousing the grass with gasoline. We had barely the time to run to the border of the dense forest, which the fire could not burn.

In our escape we forgot about the little orphan. I tried to convince myself he had fled like us. But, alas, he had stayed with his mother, perhaps hoping that she would get up and help him escape. He was crying, screaming, but he did not run away, though he must have been blinded and smothered by the smoke. When the flames touched him, he screamed.

I heard his squealing. I wanted to run back, perhaps do something to get him out of this inferno or at worst to shoot him in the head to end his suffering. But the flames were too high and the heat unbearable. I could not see him, but two or three times I still heard his plaintive cries, then nothing but the crackling of the fire. In just a few moments the wildfire had transformed the savanna into a bare, black, and fuming place.

I walked on ground covered with hot ashes and a few still-burning twigs. A strong odor of burned fat was in the hot air. I looked for the bush where the female elephant had lain, but it was gone. In its place were a few branches like a scrawny hand pointing black fingers toward the sky ... and two charred masses, the bodies of my elephants. The baby had taken refuge between his mother's legs for the last suck of milk. Like her, he was horribly burned. She was dead, but he was still breathing. I came close to him and saw his tongue still wet and red. His eyelids, tinged with blood, were open and he looked at me, seeing the assassin that I was, although he extended his trunk in my direction as if for a last handshake. I took it in my hand. Burned skin stuck to my palm. I shot him in the head. I was trembling, shaken by waves of cold as if suffering an attack of malaria. I went behind a tree to vomit uncontrollably.

Never will I be able to forget that little animal's shrill, plaintive screams of pain followed by little cries that sounded like sobs, mixed with the infernal sounds of burning dry grass and bamboo branches exploding in the searing heat. Never will I forget that baby's round eyes crying for his mother, and his last tearless, accusing stare.

It was at that moment that I swore to myself that I would never hunt again, that I would do all in my power to convince other hunters to give up their pastime and instead do something useful for animals.

Even now, after so many years, I am still haunted by the little elephant. I see again that tragic scene in my mind's eye, and feel a pain in my chest at the memory of his sweet, sad stare. It is a memory that will stay with me forever.

# In the Footsteps of Frederick Courteney Selous

## Chapter 18

In order for the reader to understand the political situation in South Vietnam fully and how it affected big-game hunting in that country, I have to go many years back in time.

Two years after the victory of the Viet Minh at Dien Bien Phu (1954), which resulted in the partition of Vietnam into two entities, the north and the south, the new government of South Vietnam took its revenge on the French colonists who had humiliated the natives for nearly two hundred years. The French were fired from all the jobs that could be performed by Vietnamese. This decree especially hurt the young soldiers of the "Corps Expéditionnaire" who had settled in the country after being demobilized. Most of them had native common-law wives and children.

The loss of jobs put them into the category of undesirable loiterers and thus eligible for deportation. Their return to France would be paid for by the French administration, but if they wanted their families to accompany them, the soldiers would have to pay their way. Many could not afford this expense and would have to leave their loved ones behind. To stay in the country, many disappeared and became outlaws, living clandestinely on the opium traffic or through deals they made on the black market. The majority were caught and jailed in the Chi Hoa prison, where they waited for the French administration to come up with enough money to take care of their deportation.

Another decree aiming at hurting the French was the confiscation of their weapons—the same restriction the French formerly applied to the Vietnamese. During French supremacy, only a few upper-class Vietnamese were granted permission to possess a weapon, which was often a hunting smoothbore. Very few natives were authorized to have rifled guns. Therefore, hunting was out of reach for the Vietnamese. During all the time I lived in South Vietnam, I knew only five or six native hunters. No more than one hundred guns were in the hands of the Vietnamese, Cambodians, and Laotians. I obtained that information in 1960 from a man who hunted sometimes with me and worked for the Vietnamese Sureté.

After the coup of 9 March 1945, I had to surrender all my guns to the Japanese. Since French law required that all owners of weapons be given a permit to carry firearms, it was easy for the Japanese to have the names of all gun owners. I got my weapons back after Japan's defeat—but not for long. Vietnam became independent after Dien Bien Phu and took its revenge on all Frenchmen, who again had to return their firearms.

At that time I organized a tourist-based hunting company, called Sladang Safari, that soon gained an excellent reputation with its many foreign clients and thus brought in currency that Vietnam needed. Consequently, I was given permission to keep two rifles. I worked with my clients only during the dry season. The rest of the year was the monsoon season when it was too humid and soggy for people to walk through the jungle in pursuit of wild animals. This was the period I chose to replenish my stock of ivory, tiger and panther skins, and gaur horns. I sold them to hunters who wanted additional trophies. I can say without boasting that almost all the tiger skins and elephant tusks bought by foreign hunters during the years 1957–1962 came from me.

Seeing the success of my business, a few French and Vietnamese amateurs decided to launch hunting companies. Their mistake was promising unrealistic results, such as one or two tigers, a gaur, an Asiatic buffalo, and a banteng—not to mention a kouprey and one or two panthers—in just thirty days in the field. Some even promised a black panther! It wasn't long before their frustrated clients flooded their embassies with complaints. To avoid being arrested for breach of contract, the dishonest hunter–guides disappeared into neighboring Cambodia or Laos for a few weeks until they felt it was safe to resurface.

I stuck to the clauses of my contracts, however, and kept all my promises, so my clients from the United States, France, and Italy spoke highly of me once back in their countries, and I was flooded with demands for safaris during the years 1957–1962.

The success of Sladang Safari made many hunters jealous. One of them was the guide for Mr. Nhu, brother of and adviser to President Ngo Dinh Diem, who loved hunting. He told his powerful client that I was a danger to the government and that I should not be allowed to keep any guns. He said I used my hunting company as a pretext to travel to the borders of Cambodia and Laos to meet Montagnard rebels and train them to become snipers. Snipers would make it unsafe for Mr. Nhu to hunt in the jungle. He also said that I was often seen with agents of the CIA and France's Military Intelligence. As the last drop in his almost overflowing vase of accusations, he added that I was the companion of Lechi, Madame Nhu's sister. Mr. Nhu, accustomed to having many political enemies, might have ignored my alleged activities against the regime, but he certainly bristled at this last piece of information.

However, I could no longer hunt since my guns had been confiscated. I was also watched discreetly. I felt doomed to an anguishing future. My first move was to get enough money to settle in another country. I had to sell my little farm, and my hunting and farming vehicles and other equipment. Many people made offers. They knew they could take advantage of my desperate situation to get most of my things at a bargain price.

I had spent all my life in Vietnam, much of it in the jungle on the tracks of wild animals. I had no fear of people with a reputation for being dangerous. I never hesitated to follow a wounded tiger and give it the coup de grace to shorten its suffering, although a few hunters had been killed doing so. I had run before charging cow elephants because I did not want to kill the females. My Montagnard trackers had seen me take risks to avoid killing needlessly. This was my way of life. Where could I find a place to lead the same simple existence? I would not know how to live in a city.

One of my American clients, who was aware of my problems, offered to put me in contact with a professional hunting guide in Gabon. I thought perhaps this was the solution. I started to read books about big-game hunting on the African continent. One of them was by Frederick C. Selous, a famous professional white hunter who described his hunts in East Africa with an old-fashioned gun during the last quarter of the nineteenth century. Maybe I could find a similar old gun and start a campaign to acquire ivory as Selous did.

I remembered the oath I had made to myself after having to kill the baby elephant I found dying in a forest fire. I had felt so guilty that I had sworn never to kill another elephant again. But my present situation would force me to violate my oath, for to live decently in another country, I needed the money that ivory could bring. I was outraged at the thought that I owed all my problems to that neurotic woman who dominated the Diem government.

While trying to find that old gun, I continued my reading on big-game hunting in Africa. I realized that those hunters for whom I had a lot of admiration had not been supermen—they had lived in an epoch of wildlife abundance that allowed them to shoot as many elephants as they wanted. Their hunts were massacres of males, females, and young—anything with 7 to 50 kilos (15 to 110 pounds) of ivory. On any given day they killed from ten to twenty beasts. They were poachers like myself, the only difference being that I had a permit to hunt and they did not need one.

The information in the books by the famous African hunters contained some contradictions. Selous said that in 1874 tusks weighing 60 to 70 pounds were very rare, while W. D. M. "Karamojo" Bell, Marcus Daly, and John Hunter, whose careers took place later, in the years 1890–1910, wrote that their bulls had ivory weighing 35 to 80 pounds per tusk, and sometimes they took bulls whose tusks weighed 170 to as much as 215 pounds each.

With my big-game experience, I realized that many among those great hunters were nervous when approaching a herd of elephants, and shot indiscriminately at any animals having tusks, be they male or female. What I admired, however, was their insane courage. They faced elephants and rhinos with one-shot muskets loaded with minimally controlled doses of black powder propelling big balls of lead; these loads lacked accuracy and penetrating power. Besides, those muskets, weighing thirteen to seventeen pounds, could dislocate a man's shoulder when fired. The hunters needed great physical strength to carry their guns over long distances, in addition to great courage and will power. I would not like to use such weapons, but I believe I would not have behaved differently if I had lived in those times. The introduction of pyroxylin [smokeless] powder, cordite, and solid bullets have contributed to the safety and effectiveness of hunters over the years.

For days my quest for an old gun remained unsuccessful. One morning, as I began to despair, luck took my side. As I was shopping in the market of Da Lat, I met Charles Vally, an old friend who had participated in my training as a hunter by the Montagnard guide K'Loi and his sons. Charles was a tea planter, but he also hunted occasionally. He had seen me shoot green pigeons in flight with my .22 Long Rifle. Impressed by my precision, he had invited me to participate in his hunts for ivory. We had hunted together in areas which had never been troubled by the shots of firearms. Several times he had seen me kill two or three elephants running away. He had nicknamed me the "reincarnation of Karamojo Bell," since I hunted with a 7mm Mauser and used solid Kynoch ammunition.

The market was a place in the center of the city where one could find a French restaurant next to a Chinese restaurant, a tea room with the best cakes in the world, a library containing French classics, a beauty salon, a pawn shop, and small eating places where one could get tasty Vietnamese or Chinese soups. A motley mixture of half-naked Montagnards and elegant tourists from Saigon meandered among stands of fresh flowers, vegetables, fish and other foods, and displays of silk or cotton materials. Anyone having something to sell simply sat on the sidewalk and displayed his merchandise in baskets.

In this marketplace one could also hear the latest rumors. Charles, of course, had heard about my expulsion. We decided to sit in the quiet eatery of an old Chinese man who still had a few bottles of Nuit St. Georges wine. I told him about my intention of going on an ivory campaign to get enough money to settle in another country after my expulsion. I explained that I could not even think of selling wild game meat because it would be easy for the government to find out about my poaching activities. Ivory, however, would be more difficult to trace. I knew many Americans in Saigon who would be eager to buy elephant tusks. I also had the address of a Chinese trader who bought and sold ivory clandestinely. When investigators asked about the source of his ivory, he always said he bought it from Khmer or Laotian merchants. He was well known by the Vietnamese government, so nobody could involve me in the traffic. Charles asked whether I had a weapon for this project.

"No," I replied. "I am looking for any old or new gun."

"Well, go home. Take with you a few hunting clothes, two pairs of boots, some money, and come to my plantation for a few days. I think I'll have something for you, but don't say anything to anyone about your stay at my place."

I told Lechi that I would have to be absent for a few weeks to take care of important business concerning my expulsion. I would have to go alone because her presence would attract too much attention and perhaps abort the deal. She did not insist on having more details or accompanying me. She let me move freely about, knowing perfectly well that I would eventually confide in her. She only reminded me to be prudent: "Don't forget that your enemies are watching you."

It was a pleasure to find myself again in the rough hunting ambiance of Charles's bungalow. All the anxiety caused by my precarious situation disappeared as I talked about past hunts and drank good red Sahel wine and nibbled dried and spicy deer meat with a friend who understood the excitement of tracking wild animals. After a while Charlie disappeared into his workroom and returned with a double-barrel 10-gauge shotgun with 32-inch half-choke barrels. Made on order by a Belgian gunsmith, it had external hammers, a beautiful stock in old walnut, bluing on the barrels that was still very visible, and a gray-colored breech. Charlie handed it to me. It was heavy, about 11 pounds, but it felt good in my hands.

Charlie explained that he had been able to keep the gun because it never did have a permit. From time to time he sent his old guide on a night hunt for a sambar. Some Montagnards had worked for him for twenty years, and he considered them more like friends than employees. They returned his trust in them and loved him like their own father. They had never betrayed him by talking about the gun.

"I have killed several tigers, a few gaurs, and tens of wild oxen with it," Charlie told me. "I have never tried it on an elephant, however. You will be the first one to do that. I have round lead bullets especially made for elephants, and ammunition loaded with buckshot. In addition I have fifty new copper cases, 2 kilos (4½ pounds) of black powder, and all the equipment to reload them. I only lack good cylindrical bullets like the Brenneke. With this kind of projectile, you can kill your elephant from a distance of 30 meters (100 feet) as surely as with your .404 or your 7mm Mauser. With this musket you will be following right along in the footsteps of Selous, who was armed with his 10-gauge, one-shot loaded with black powder and bullets as big as golf balls. Of course, you have an advantage over him in this gun's penetration power and accuracy, and you can shoot twice instead of only once.

"If the gun suits you, take it. I'll trade it for your first pair of tusks, no matter their size. My only condition is that you never mention my name. If the police arrest you, this weapon is yours. You can use it and trust my guides. They will help you avoid villages and bad encounters. They will do the tracking and the carrying of trophies for you. Treat them the way you would old friends. They will respect you and trust you when I tell them about your past as a hunter. What do you say?"

What unexpected good fortune! I accepted my old friend's offer. Charlie went again to his workroom and returned with two boxes of solid bullets for .465 Holland & Holland. He put them on the table with a notebook and a pencil.

"We are going to create a new bullet. I recently read in the *Popular Mechanics* journal that in the United States a new type of bullet has been put on the market for smoothbore hunting guns. It is called the 'sabot.' I have been thinking about it, and you arrived just at the moment I decided to fabricate my new bullets."

The next morning I heard him moving back in his workroom. He was digging round holes 3 centimeters (1³⁄₁₆ inches) deep in a 10-centimeter (4-inch)-thick wooden beam. The holes were the size of 10-gauge slugs. He centered the .465 bullets in the bottom of the holes, which he filled to the one-third level with melted lead. Once the metal had cooled, he poured the contents of his "mold" onto the table—these were the projectiles for my ivory campaign. They had the shape of rubber nipples used as pacifiers for babies. The base of the .465 projectile was encircled to one-third of its height with a 10-gauge lead ring, whose purpose was to keep the bullet on a steady trajectory. Once it hit a target, the ring would fall away and the bullet would continue its course into the animal.

We went out to test our new rocket. The results were more than satisfactory. At distances of 10 to 50 yards I could place my bullet into a 2½-foot-square target. The projectile could penetrate a pine tree as deeply as 15 inches. I did not need a more powerful weapon to kill even a running elephant. I was impatient to start experimenting. We went to Cordier's French restaurant, the only one in the area, to celebrate our success with a good meal and a few bottles of wine.

The old guide and his sons had followed us for the testing, and they were all excited at the thought of hunting again with their boss.

"We hunt elephants with the new bullets?" they asked Charlie.

"No," he replied. "I am too old now for this sport. The bullets are for Mr. Etienne. I'll explain to you after lunch."

When we came back from lunch they were waiting for us in front of the bungalow. My friend explained the whole situation to them:

"You must not tell anyone about the testing of the new bullets. It is forbidden by the government. If the police know what we have done, we'll go to jail. I am giving the gun to Mr. Etienne, and he is the one who will hunt the elephants. If you want, you and your sons may go with him to guide him, and carry his supplies and trophies. He will go in the direction of Phan Thiet behind the plantation. You will be well paid, and you will receive a bonus for each elephant with tusks weighing more than 15 kilos (33 pounds). But remember, you must keep a complete silence on the hunt because the French are no longer allowed to kill elephants. No one must know that Mr. Etienne has come here. No talking even to your wives."

After they left, I asked Charlie whether we could trust them. He told me they had never revealed the existence of the gun since the coup of 9 March 1945. They had even hidden it along with a 12-gauge Darne from the Japanese.

"If the Vietnamese government asks about the sudden absence of the men, we'll say that they are guiding American hunters. The Americans can have the guns they want and go hunting when they want." Charlie said this last with some bitterness.

"Charlie," I said, "I'll go on my ivory campaign right from your plantation. I don't have the time to go back to Da Lat to tell my friend Lechi. Could you please tell her to come in two weeks to get me on the trail near the plantation?"

Charlie understood that I could keep no secrets from Lechi and he promised to tell her. My good friend Charlie took big risks in helping me, and I will never forget it. I hunted in the region of Bryan and the good places he knew there. Every other week he went with Lechi on the trail, which had not been used for a long time. He loaded into his Jeep the tusks I had buried nearby, and we relaxed for a few days in his bungalow.

I was lucky enough to kill seven elephants with tusks weighing over 22 kilos (48 pounds) each, and a dozen animals with tusks of 8 to 12 kilos

(17 to 26 pounds). My campaign ended in the region of Djiring. After three months of hunting, hundreds of kilometers of marching through the jungle, and contacts with dozens of elephant herds, I was happy to sleep in my bed and take long baths in my tub.

After a few days' rest, I made plans to hunt in other regions such as Krong Pha, Taloo, Manoï, and Bidup—regions not important enough to be indicated on a map—that I knew well, but I was careful to stay far away from the villages and the trails. My carriers were four guides from Lang Bian, friends from my childhood. My tracker was an expert with whom I had often hunted in the past. I had given him a .303 Enfield gun, but his friends had talked about it and the Vietnamese government confiscated it and put its owner in jail for three months. Once released, he went back to his tracking job. I stayed in that region for two weeks each time; then Lechi came to pick me up. With or without ivory, I waited for her on a previously agreed upon date. I got a few good trophies but none with tusks over 20 kilos (44 pounds).

My last campaign took place near R'Pouma Klong, an area already crowded with the Viet Cong. I knew, however, that they would leave me alone—they were busy getting ready to overthrow the hated Diem government. There I was lucky enough to kill an elephant with tusks of 35 kilos (77 pounds) and several other bulls with smaller tusks.

The end of my extended stay was approaching—I had to leave the country within two months. After paying all my hunting expenses, I still had a small fortune that would allow me to live for many months without financial worries. I was able to sell only my Jeeps and my Fiat tractor. After I left, all that remained of my farm disappeared: The equipment, the poultry, the rabbits, and the pigs were stolen by refugees from North Vietnam, Diem's protégés, who lived nearby. They even ate my five dogs, in spite of my keeper's attempts to stop them.

I was about to return Charlie's musket to him when I heard about his sudden death from heart failure. He had been sick for a long time without knowing it. I greased his gun and wrapped it in a special material made with rubber truck tubes. Then I put the whole package into a metal box that I hid under the roof of my house. I am sure that Charlie's gun is still there.

I calmly awaited the date of my deportation. I had chosen Cambodia as my new country because it was just across Vietnam's border. I hoped to return to my former life after the fall of the Ngo government. Rumors were circulating that an imminent coup was going to end Diem's regime and all his clique would be publicly hanged. Alas, that impatiently awaited event would come too late: The Ngo brothers—Diem, Nhu, and Can—were assassinated on 3 November 1963. Their deaths could no longer change anything for me.

Only two weeks before the date of my deportation, I was kidnapped from my farm one morning at 7 A.M. Several soldiers handcuffed me before taking me by airplane to Saigon, where they threw me in an underground jail controlled by a man named Tuyen, a Himmler in miniature but much more sadistic. There I was harassed with lack of sleep and water, thanks to the hateful orders of my future sister-in-law, Madame Nhu, and her brother Khiem, who had been my friend from childhood. To ensure Khiem's support, she had given him a small position in the government, and he had become as arrogant and cruel as she. He was so devoid of moral principles that he went to the point of killing his own parents, beating them to death in their house in Washington, D.C., in 1986.

After two weeks of harassment in the secret jail, they took me to Cambodia without allowing me to say good-bye to my mother, who cried at the gate of the jail. I had barely crossed the border when I came down with cholera, probably the result of an overdose of vaccine administered to me in jail by Dr. Tuyen's nurses. To my surprise and distress, the city hospital of Phnom Penh refused to admit me since I was not a resident there. After I called the French Consulate, which refused to answer for me, a hospital official suggested that I go to a private clinic managed by a Hungarian Communist doctor. It was not difficult for me to understand that the French Diplomatic Corps in Cambodia had been influenced by the French ambassador in Vietnam, who had decided not to provoke Madame Nhu's anger by helping me—even though he knew perfectly well that I was very sick and in danger of being assassinated by her hit men.

After spending three weeks in the capital of the Khmer kingdom, I took a plane to the United States, where Lechi was waiting for me in her parents' house. I was finally safe and sound, but still eaten by anxiety: How could I manage to earn a living in a country whose language I did not speak well? And what job could I obtain in the cities, given that I had always lived and worked in the jungle?

Later I realized that fate had been good to me. God had allowed my gold to be taken away in order to replace it with a diamond, Lechi, who has been my wife now for forty-eight years.

The coup that destroyed the Ngo regime came on 3 November 1963, the anniversary date of my departure from Indochina a year earlier. I found that coincidence troubling, for it was as if Nemesis, the goddess of vengeance, had whispered to me, "I have allowed you to take your revenge." If I were one of those rotten people who had managed to avoid punishment after the coup, I would not live with peace of mind because divine justice always strikes sooner or later.

# A Foolproof Gun
## Chapter 19

I have been often asked what I consider to be the ideal arm for big-game hunting, a gun-of-all-work, a "master gun" for general hunting. It is difficult to make such a choice because each hunter has his favorites. Some say that the Winchester .405 Model 1895 is the ideal hunting rifle. The Marquis de Monestrol, the well-known and scholarly author of *La Faune et la Flore Indochinoises (Animals and Plants in Indochina),* swore by this gun, which he used to kill numerous gaurs, bantengs, elephants, and more than one hundred tigers. The Marquis claimed "... half a century of hunting [big game] without any problems of mechanics, misfires, and with the Kynoch solids." Other hunters, however, have claimed that this weapon was an antique, good only for wounding animals. They preferred the British big-bore expresses with two barrels, such as Westley Richards, Holland & Holland, or Rigby.

During much of my hunting career, I swore only by the commercial Mauser Oberndorf. I used all the Mausers—the 5.5, 7mm, 8mm, 9mm, 9.3x62, 10.75x68, and .404 Jeffery—and never had any problems. The best ammunition, in my opinion, was Kynoch.

I started my career as a hunter with military guns—Martini-Henry, 8mm Lebel, 7x57, 8x57 Mauser, .303 Enfield, .30-06 Springfield, and Garand .30 U.S. caliber. My preferred calibers were the 7x57 and the .30-06. The secondhand rifles I bought never disappointed me because I chose them very carefully. Ammunition was easier to find for those than for the big hunting calibers. I had to give up the one I liked best, the .404 Jeffery Mauser, because I could not find ammunition for it. I replaced it with a .375 H&H Francotte, made by a Belgian gunsmith. It had a Krupp barrel mounted on a Mauser Magnum action. I used only Mauser rifles or others made to order with Mauser Oberndorf commercial actions.

It is easy to understand why the Mauser action outstrips all the others in the minds of many hunters. Gunsmiths throughout the world used the Mauser Oberndorf action in creating the masterpieces of English, German, and Belgian rifle manufacture. All the elegant, foolproof, finely finished rifles that every hunter dreamed of possessing were endowed with the Mauser. Even the Rival, a gun manufactured in St. Etienne, France, was well known by colonial hunters; it was the only French-made rifle with such a good reputation.

First it was the 10.75 Mauser, then later the .375 H&H, a gun mounted on a Mauser Magnum Oberndorf breech. A few U.S. gunsmiths did the same thing with their weapons, creating masterpieces comparable to those of other countries. In my opinion, the best hunting guns made in the United States came from Hoffman or Griffin & Howe. In 1950 I owned a .505 Gibbs manufactured by Hoffman. It was a marvel. Unfortunately, the ammunition often misfired, and it was nearly impossible to find cartridges in that caliber on the market. I replaced it with a 10.75x68 Mauser.

Price was the reason so few hunters had the weapon of their dreams. Caffort, the only arms dealer in Saigon, South Vietnam, and Phnom Penh, Cambodia, sold a .350 Rigby or a .375 H&H for about $550 U.S.; a Mauser of the same caliber sold for $150 in 1940. Those English guns were perfect: The finish, the bluing on the metal, the marbling of the breech, the gunstock wood, the aiming system, and the Mauser breech were above criticism. Except for its more modest looks, the Mauser was no slouch either. I must confess, however, that I would have chosen the elegant British weapons if I could have afforded them. Nonetheless, the Mauser had its own character and a distinctive line that hunters all over the world immediately recognized and appreciated.

Alas, we shall no longer see this marvelous rifle used wherever there is big-game hunting. I am referring to the real commercial Mauser Oberndorf of 1905–1938, not the ersatz versions with Mauser-style breeches manufactured by unknown factories. Here is a list of the weapons and calibers I often used during my twenty-two years of hunting small, medium, and big game in South Vietnam:

A) 1920 Mauser Oberndorf 5.5, .22 Long Rifle, with five-cartridge magazine, used for small game, birds included.

B) Mauser Oberndorf 7x57 commercial carbine, used with Kynoch solid and soft ammunition for medium game.

C) .404 Mauser Magnum breech with a flat top, used with Kynoch solid and soft ammunition for big game.

For both hunting and my own personal protection, I used a U.S. 30-caliber M1A1 carbine with a folding stock, and for it I had ten magazines, each holding fifteen cartridges. It could be used on wild boar, deer, for the finishing shot on game, and to protect the camp. It was used during the years 1945–1961, when the Viet Minh and the Viet Cong represented a real danger. That rifle provided good firepower. In addition to the guns, I always took on hunts a bag containing five or six U.S.-made hand grenades, which I used most often to stun fish in rivers.

Since the destruction of the Mauser factories in Oberndorf, Germany, during World War II, hunters all over the world have waited for the reappearance of the wonderful guns made from 1920 to 1942. They will wait in vain, I am afraid, because I am certain now that Mauser will never again make these outstanding weapons of the past.

I have felt compelled to write my memoirs as a professional hunter in Vietnam because I wanted to share with hunters all over the world the joys that the Vietnam of yesteryear had given me.

Since I left that country in November 1962, I have never been tempted to go back, although Vietnam is now open to tourists. I have heard that luxurious thirty-story hotels have been built, that their employees speak mostly English or Russian, and that only old people can still understand French. Although I have not forgotten the Vietnamese language and could still communicate easily with the natives, I have the feeling that I would be like a stranger in that country where I was born.

I have heard that the Montagnards have been integrated into the Vietnamese population and that the jungle has been transformed into national parks. I suppose that the wild animals have either been destroyed or relocated to zoos. The hunting paradise of my youth exists only in my memory. That is why I am writing this book—so that, for a few hours, my wonderful jungle might again become alive for my readers.

# Glossary

# Glossary

## Characters

**Bao Dai:** Last emperor of Vietnam; deposed by Ngo Dinh Diem in 1956; Lechi's cousin.

**Brooks, Berry B.:** Client of the author who had the reputation of being one of the world's greatest hunters; wealthy cotton farmer.

**Da Cruz, François and Jean:** Author's childhood friends.

**Diem, Ngo Dinh:** President of South Vietnam 1956–1963; supported by the United States; assassinated in a coup by the military.

**Hansen, Gerhard:** Scientist who discovered the causative agent of leprosy.

**K'Loi:** Old Montagnard guide, father of K'Sou and K'War.

**K'Put:** K'War's wife.

**K'Sou and K'War:** Young Montagnard hunting guides and childhood friends of the author.

**Lechi:** Client of the author in 1960 and the first Vietnamese woman to kill a tiger and a spotted panther; wife of the author.

**Millet, Fernand:** French wildlife official in 1919, known as an expert in the art of hunting; author of the book *Les Grands Animaux Sauvages de l'Annam.*

**Monestrol, Marquis de:** French colonist, known as "the 100 tiger man"; author of the very good book *La Flore et la Faune Indochinoises.*

**Nhu, Madame:** First lady of South Vietnam; Lechi's sister.

**Viet Minh:** Revolutionary movement fighting against France for Vietnam's independence, 1941–1954.

**Tran, Dr. Van Chuong:** Ambassador of South Vietnam to Washington D.C. 1953–1962; Lechi's father.

**Tran, Princess Nam:** Wife of Dr. Van Chuong Tran; ambassador to the United Nations 1953–1962; Lechi's mother.

## Cities, Villages, and Other Places in South Vietnam

**Cagne:** Well-known hunting region in Djiring province.

**Ban Dong:** Province in South Vietnam with a high percentage of Montagnard population.

**Ban Me Thuot:** Province in South Vietnam.

**Bidup, Mont:** Chain of mountains between Da Lat and Nha Trang (city on the seashore).

**Blao:** Small town in South Vietnam.

**Bross Deur:** Small Montagnard village near the Da Dung River.

**Bryan:** Mountain near Djiring.

**Cam Ly:** Hunting region near Da Lat.

**Ca Na:** Salt marsh near Phan Ráng, South Vietnam.

**Cu Chi:** Area in South Vietnam well known for its aquatic game hunting; during the 1961–1970 war involving the United States, the Viet Cong (southern guerrillas) built an underground city there that allowed them to live under a U.S. military base.

**Da Dung, Da Huai, La Lagna, Da Nhim, Song Pha, Song Mao:** Rivers in South Vietnam.

**Da Lat:** Resort mountain city on the high plateau of Lang Bian.

**Dam Rong:** Montagnard village near Ban Me Thuot.

**Dar Lac:** Province in South Vietnam.

**Dinh Quan:** Former military post at milestone 113 on Saigon–Da Lat highway.

**Djiring:** Plateau and small town in South Vietnam.

**Dông Mé:** Village in South Vietnam.

**Dran Pass:** Small town and railroad station between Krong Pha and Da Lat.

**Gia Bac:** Forest trail from Djiring to Phan Thiet.

**Gia Lam:** Railroad station near Phan Thiet.

**Ka La:** Small Montagnard village six miles from Djiring; famous for its hospital for lepers.

**Khe Sanh:** U.S. military base 1961–1970.

**Khmer Kingdom:** Cambodia.

**Kon Tum:** Province in South Vietnam.

**Krong Pha:** Hunting region in South Vietnam.

**Nam Banh:** Village in South Vietnam.

**Nha Trang:** Seaside city near Da Lat.

**Pleiku:** Province in South Vietnam.

**Ratanakiri:** Province in Cambodia.

**Riong Serignac:** Montagnard village.

**R'Pouma Klong:** Montagnard village.

**Tan My:** Village in South Vietnam.

## Animals, Vegetation, and Other Natural Elements

**Bait:** A dead animal attached to a tree near a blind to attract tigers or panthers.

**Bang-lang:** Tree of South Vietnam.

**Banteng:** Wild ox of Vietnam and Cambodia.

**Dâtches:** Salty lands or swamps, necessary to animal life.

**Dâu:** Red oak tree whose wood is popular for construction of houses.

**Gaur:** Large bovine of Vietnam, a prized hunting trophy, that has black skin with white legs.

**Kouprey:** A wild ox, frequenting the forests of Vietnam and Cambodia.

**Krait:** Highly poisonous snake.

**Mirador:** French for hunting blind, a small camouflage-covered shelter in which a hunter awaits his prey.

**Muntjac:** Small deer, also called *chevreuil* in French and *con mån* in Vietnamese.

**Pastis:** Typical French drink made from the essence of anise, or *badiane*, which was much appreciated by old Indochinese colonists.

**Rays:** Mountain rice fields.

**Sambar:** Deer of Southeast Asia.

**Seladang:** Indonesian name for gaur.

**Tranh:** Tall grass in the savannas, used to roof huts.

**Tra-num:** Fermented rice alcohol, the Montagnards' beer.

**Trousse-couilles:** A band of blue cloth attached to a belt men wore between their legs. It served as a brief and a sarong.

**Velvet horn:** Deer shed their antlers at a certain time each year. When they grow back, the antlers are soft and covered with a fine "fur." Chinese druggists believe in the aphrodisiac qualities of those soft antlers and use them in their medicine. Soft antlers from deer are also used today in medicine in the United States and Europe.

## Guns and Ammunition

**Berthier:** French light carbine, originally made in 1892.

**Brenneke and J. R.:** The best slugs for shotguns.

**Express Double:** Large-caliber, two-barrel gun for big game.

**Holland & Holland .375 :** Expensive double rifle made in England for hunting.

**Lebel:** French rifle, originally made in 1886.

**Martini-Henry:** The first Empire service rifle, used by the English in Africa during the wars against the Zulus in 1870 and the Boers in 1902.

**Mauser Oberndorf 8x60 and .404:** German hunting guns made between 1905 and 1938, and used by the author for small game.

**War weapons:** U.S. .30 caliber M1A1 carbine, .303 Enfield, .30-06 Springfield and Garand, SKS-M16, M14, AK-47. These rifles, made in U.S., England, Russia, or China, were frequently used by natives in Vietnam.

**Winchester Model 70 in .22 Hornet:** Rifle used for small game.

SAFARI PRESS